WITHDRAWN
UTSA Libraries

BURT FRANKLIN: RESEARCH & SOURCE WORKS SERIES 560
Selected Essays in History, Economics, & Social Science 180

FOREIGN
VISITORS IN ENGLAND

FOREIGN
VISITORS IN ENGLAND

AND

What they have Thought of Us

BEING

*SOME NOTES ON THEIR BOOKS AND THEIR OPINIONS
DURING THE LAST THREE CENTURIES.*

BY

EDWARD SMITH

**BURT FRANKLIN
NEW YORK**

Published by LENOX HILL Pub. & Dist. Co. (Burt Franklin)
235 East 44th St., New York, N.Y. 10017
Originally Published: 1889
Reprinted: 1970
Printed in the U.S.A.

S.B.N. 8337-32978
Library of Congress Card Catalog No.: 77-132688
Burt Franklin: Research and Source Works Series 560
Selected Essays in History, Economics, and Social Science 18

INTRODUCTION.

T will be seen, from the ensuing pages, that there is material for very curious and interesting inquiry in the opinions and experiences of travellers in Great Britain.

The frequent re-perusal of the memoirs of such travellers leads one to see that there is 'a good deal of human nature' about Englishmen; and that we have a special force of character, which brings us to extremes of both bad and good. We are, without doubt, difficult to understand on first acquaintance. The reason is this: that the average foreigner comes armed with prejudices. But when at last a Frenchman, or a Dutchman, or a German has succeeded in penetrating the character and understanding something of the habits and modes of thought of the ordinary English gentleman, he is first impelled to admire, and at length to love.

Among our intelligent visitors, there are some who are disposed to indulge the best hopes for England's welfare; whilst a very great number have reached our shores with their minds overweighted with the prejudices of their own fatherland. As for those of our own day, some have deliberately come as apostles of their own notions: the peace-and-equality fad, the anti-slavery fad, the women's rights fad, etc., are in turn flaunted in our face. This is especially so with American visitors. In these cases, the objects and advantages of a trip to London are so far missed, in that they do not minister to the special fancies of system-mongers.

The following essay is chiefly devoted to some visitors of the seventeenth and eighteenth centuries; although some references are made to diarists of our own and the last generation. When the reader learns that the bibliography of the subject

Introduction. vii

extends to at least four hundred items, he will readily understand that an exhaustive treatment of the subject would exceed the modest limits at our disposal.

As far as we are aware, there has been but one serious endeavour previously to present a picture of England collected from the writings of foreigners, viz.: 'England as seen by Foreigners in the Days of Elizabeth and James I. . . . By WILLIAM BRENCHLEY RYE, assistant keeper of the department of printed books, British Museum.' London, 1865. It would be impossible to praise too highly the execution of this work: a marvel of erudition and good taste. The exceptional opportunities enjoyed by Mr. Rye, supplemented by his own excellent linguistic and historical attainments, have here enabled us to come face to face with society during this interesting period in our annals, concerning many matters on which the native annalist is often silent.

BIBLIOGRAPHY OF THE WORKS QUOTED IN THIS VOLUME.

VON ROZMITAL.—A Bohemian noble (*circa* 1466). Quoted from W. B. Rye.
    [First published at Olmütz in 1577. The *Quarterly Review* of March, 1852 (xc., pp. 413-444), has an article under the title of 'Bohemian Embassy to England, Spain, etc., in 1466,' in which the more interesting passages from this curious work are given at large.]

GRUTHUYSE.—'Narratives of the Arrival of Louis de Bruges, Seigneur de la Gruthuyse, in England, and of his creation as Earl of Winchester, in 1472.' Published in *Archæologia*, xxvi. 265-286.
    [From Additional MSS. 6113. Edward IV. had been entertained and befriended by this grandee when in exile; and this journal relates the efforts made by Edward to honour him publicly at Court and elsewhere.]

TREVISANO.—'A Relation, or rather a True Account of the Island of England . . . about the year 1500.' *Camden Society*, 1847.
    [Andrea Trevisano, ambassador to England in 1497.]

GIUSTINIAN.—'Four Years at the Court of Henry VIII. Selection of despatches written by the Venetian Ambassador, Sebastian Giustinian, and addressed to the Signory of Venice, January 12, 1515, to July 26, 1519. Translated by Rawdon Brown.' 2 vols., 8vo., London, 1854.

NICANDER NUCIUS.—'The Second Book of the Travels of Nicander Nucius. Edited from the original Greek MS. in the Bodleian Library, with an English translation by the Rev. J. A. Cramer, D.D.' *Camden Society*, 1841.

[Supposed to be in the suite of an embassy to England, 1545-6.]

PERLIN.—'Description of England and Scotland. By Stephen Perlin' (? 1553). Translated and printed in Grose's *Antiquarian Repertory*, iv., pp. 501 *et seq*.

[First published in Paris, 1558. Reprinted, London, 1775, with an English preface. Nothing else is known of the author.]

VAN METEREN.—The Dutch historian, and sometime a merchant in London (*circa* 1558-1612). Quoted from W. B. Rye.

LEMNIUS.—A Dutch physician (? 1560). Quoted from W. B. Rye.

HENTZNER.—'A Journey into England. By Paul Hentzner, in the year 1598.' 8vo. (Latin and English), Strawberry Hill, 1757.

[Part of the journal of a tutor, who accompanied a Silesian nobleman on an extended tour in Europe. First published at Breslau, 1617. This English portion was introduced to the English reader by Horace Walpole. Since his days it has several times been reprinted.]

SULLY.—'Memoirs of Maximilian de Bethune, Duke of Sully, Prime Minister to Henry the Great . . .'

(1603). Bohn's *French Memoirs*, 5 vols., post 8vo., London, 1856.

[Printed at the Château Sully in 1638, and published at Amsterdam. Translated into English about the middle of the eighteenth century, and since reprinted. The embassy to England occurs in the second volume of Bohn's edition. It is much to be regretted that Sully was so absorbed in the affairs of his embassy as not to have made a closer examination of England and the English, for his shrewdness and discernment concerning James I. and his courtiers are marvellous. He left our country apparently with the best impressions of us.]

BASSOMPIERRE. — 'Memoirs of the Embassy of the Marshal de Bassompierre to the Court of England, in 1626. Translated, with notes.' 8vo., London, 1819.

[The notes are by John Wilson Croker.]

LA SERRE.—'Entry of Mary de Medecis, Queen Mother of France, into England, 1638. Translated from the French by the Sieur de la Serre.' Printed in Grose's *Antiquarian Repertory*, iv., pp. 520 *et seq*.

[Printed in London, in the French language, 1639. Reprinted in 1775, in company with PERLIN, *ante*. Jean Puget de la Serre, historiographer of France, was a miscellaneous writer of somewhat ephemeral books. He is immensely pleased with his trip to England.]

SORBIÈRE.—' A Voyage to England, containing many things relating to the state of learning, religion, and other curiosities of that kingdom. By Mons. Sorbière . . .' (? 1664). 8vo., London, 1709.

[This translation professes to be the first

correct one. The work, when it first appeared (Paris, 1664), caused an immense sensation, and brought forth several 'answers.' Louis XIV. showed his displeasure by a temporary banishment of the author. Dr. Wm. King published in 1698 a humorous tract, 'A Journey to London. By Monsieur Sorbière,' which long held the reputation of being the real article, and was reprinted as such as late as 1832 (Appendix to 'Mirabeau's Letters'). Sorbière wrote several works of some reputation, and was among the then leaders of science. But a prejudice existed against him as a follower of Hobbes, whose works he had translated. He probably hit some of our shortcomings with vigour, but he was a man of more than average ability and his 'voyage' is one of the more valuable of our series. Sorbière died in 1670.]

JOREVIN.—' Description of England and Ireland, in the seventeenth century. By Jorevin' (? 1666). Printed in Grose's *Antiquarian Repertory*, iv., pp. 549 *et seq.*

[From a rare book of travels, published in Paris (1672). Nothing is known of the author. He is a sociable visitor, and shows us the popular side of English life.]

COSMO.—' Travels of Cosmo III., Grand Duke of Tuscany, through England, during the reign of King Charles II., 1669. Translated from the Italian manuscript in the Laurentian Library at Florence. . .' 4to., London, 1821.

[This is the book largely used by Macaulay for his notes on Social England in the first volume of the 'History of England.' Count

Magalotti, the writer of this journal (and secretary to the prince), was a learned Italian writer and novelist of the period. He had several English correspondents, including Somers and Newton.]

GEMELLI.—'Travels through Europe, by Dr. John Gemelli-Careri, in several letters to the Counseller Amato Danio' (1686). Printed in Churchill's *Collection of Voyages*, vi., pp. 111 *et seq.* London, 1732.

[Published at Naples, 1701. This author wrote also 'A Voyage Round the World,' which was 'not included' in Harris's *Collection*, because of his tendency to take things too much at secondhand. His notices of England are particularly interesting, but the papist is very strong in him.]

MURALT.—Letters describing the Character and Customs of the English and French Nations . . . by Mr. Muralt, a gentleman of Switzerland' (? 1696). Second edition, 8vo., London, 1726.

[Originally published at Zurich. His 'Letters' are excellent, and his habits of observation very accurate.]

MISSON.—' M. Misson's Memoirs and Observations in his Travels over England. . . . Translated by Mr. Ozell ' (? 1688-97). 8vo., London, 1719.

[H. Misson resided in England several years, and is perhaps the individual mentioned in Cooper's ' List of Protestants and Aliens.' His brother, Maximilian Misson, shared the authorship of these memoirs, and also wrote a delightful 'Voyage to Italy, etc.' Misson's 'Memoirs' first appeared at the Hague, (1698).]

LA MOTRAYE.—'Aubry de la Motraye's Travels through Europe, Asia, and into Parts of Africa . . .' (? 1721-22). 3 vols. folio, 1732.

[Considered a very accurate observer. His book was published under distinguished patronage, bearing a dedication to George I.]

VOLTAIRE.—'Letters concerning the English Nation. By Mr. De Voltaire' (1728-31). 12mo., London, 1733.

POLLNITZ.—'The Memoirs of Charles Lewis, Baron de Pollnitz, being the Observations he made in his late Travels from Prussia through Germany, Italy, France, Flanders, Holland, England, etc. . . .' (1733). Third edition, 5 vols. 12mo., London, 1745.

[Published at Liège, 1734. Pollnitz was an adventurer, or soldier of fortune. He was in London trying to get notice at Court. He was delighted with England, and calls it 'a land of good sense.' He goes into raptures over English landscape. He would give up all prospects whatever in exchange for £1,000 a year, with which to keep body and soul together in this country !]

LE BLANC.—'Letters on the English and French Nations. . . . By Monsieur l'Abbé le Blanc' (1737). 2 vols., 8vo., London, 1747.

[John Bernard le Blanc, historiographer and member of several learned academies. His 'Letters' first appeared at the Hague (1745). He stayed in England about seven years. Voltaire highly praised his book.]

DU BOCAGE.—'Letters concerning England, Holland, and Italy. By the celebrated Madame du Bocage, member of the Academies of Padua,

Bologna, Rome, and Lyons . . .' (1750). 2 vols., 16mo., London, 1770.

[This lady was a celebrated poet, and her company, when in England, was in great request. Her 'Letters' are delightful. She lived to a great age, dying in 1802.]

GROSLEY.—'A Tour to London; or, New Observations on England and its Inhabitants. By M. Grosley, F.R.S., etc. . . .' (1765). 2 vols., 8vo., London, 1772.

[Pierre Jean Grosley, a lawyer and man of letters, of great reputation in some departments of history. His 'Londres' first appeared at Lausanne (1770), and had very great success. It remained the best guide to London for thirty or forty years after.]

MORITZ.—'Travels, chiefly on Foot, through several Parts of England, in 1782. . . . By Charles P. Moritz, a literary gentleman of Berlin. . . .' 8vo., London, 1783.

[A grammarian and archæologist of some repute. He died early (age 36). His book has been reprinted in Pinkerton's *Collection*, and occurs in Cassell's 'National Library.']

SILLIMAN.—'A Journal of Travels in England, Holland, and Scotland, and of Two Passages over the Atlantic, in the years 1805 and 1806.' 2 vols., 12mo., Boston (U.S.), 1810.

[Benjamin Silliman was deputed by the trustees of Yale College to purchase books and philosophical instruments in Europe, and this 'Journal' is the result. Reprinted at Newhaven (1820), with considerable additions.]

Bibliography. xv

SIMOND.—'Journal of a Tour and Residence in Great Britain during the years 1810 and 1811. . . .' 2 vols., 8vo., Edinburgh, 1815.
  [A very agreeable, good-natured work. The author had lived long in the United States of America and was well acquainted with the English language.]

VON PÜCKLER-MUSKAU. — 'Tour in England, Ireland and France, in the years 1828 and 1829. . . . By a German Prince.' 4 vols., 8vo., London, 1832.
  ['Briefe eines Verstorbenen.' Stuttgart, 1831. A book that became deservedly popular on its appearance in England. Few writers give such a clear idea of our country and its institutions.]

VON RAUMER.—'England in 1835: being a series of letters written to friends in Germany, during a residence in London, and excursions into the provinces. By Frederick von Raumer, Professor of History at the University of Berlin. . . .' 3 vols., 8vo., London, 1836.
  ['Written (says the author) under the influence of the deepest and warmest feelings.' The book was much read in Germany. Von Raumer presently revisited England, and added two more volumes to a new edition.]

CARUS.—'The King of Saxony's Journey through England and Scotland in the year 1844. By Dr. C. G. Carus, physician to the King. . . .' 8vo., London, 1846.

HAWTHORNE.—'Passages from the English Notebooks of Nathaniel Hawthorne' (1854-57). 2 vols., 12mo., Boston (U.S.), 1870.
  [Hawthorne came to England as Consul-

General at Liverpool, sent by his friend, President Pierce. He published several writings on England and English institutions, all in a pleasant vein, and overflowing with attachment to the 'old country,' although sometimes severe on unpleasant matters which struck him more than they do ourselves, to whom they are familiar. After his death, his widow resided much in England, and died here (1871). She also wrote 'Notes on England and Italy' (New York, 1868).]

ESQUIROS.—'The English at Home. By Alphonse Esquiros. . . .' 4 vols., 8vo. London, 1861-63.

[Esquiros resided here for many years, being an exile after the *coup d'état* of December, 1851. He has triumphed over most others in his attempt to delineate the English people. The work originally appeared in the 'Revue des deux mondes,' during and after 1857 ('Angleterre et la vie Anglaise').]

HOPPIN.—'Old England; Its Scenery, Art, and People. By James M. Hoppin, professor in Yale College.' 8vo., New York, 1867.

[Professor Hoppin is one of those who boast to have bettered themselves by a trip to England. He declares that his motive for publication was to induce his countrymen to spend more time in England than they usually do, instead of only making this country a stepping-stone to the Continent.]

TAINE.—'Notes on England. By H. A. Taine.' . . . 8vo., London, 1872.

DARYL.—'Public Life in England. By Philippe Daryl. Translated by Henry Frith, and revised by the author.' 8vo., London, 1884.

CONTENTS.

CHAPTER I.

Introductory.—Royal Visitors.—Foreign Embassies.—Account of Cosmo, Prince of Tuscany, and his Visit to Charles II. - - 1

CHAPTER II.

The Stranger's arrival in England.—French Manners.—English Treatment of Strangers 26

CHAPTER III.

Inns and Innkeepers.—A Pedestrian Visit to England - - - - - - - 47

CHAPTER IV.

Praises of Kent.—Canterbury and Thomas à Beckett.—To London by Water.—The River Thames - - - - - - - 59

CHAPTER V.

The Tower of London.—The City: its Streets and Shops.—St. Paul's Cathedral.—Westminster Abbey - - - - - - 69

CHAPTER VI.

St. James's Park.—The Royal Palaces.—Theobalds.—Nonesuch.—Richmond.—Windsor.—Greenwich.—Queen Elizabeth and her Court - - - - - - - 83

CHAPTER VII.

Various Sovereigns of England.—The Houses of Parliament.—Political liberty of the English people - - - - - - - 100

CHAPTER VIII.

Our National Character - - - - - 122

CHAPTER IX.

Our National Character—*continued* - - 142

CHAPTER X.

Sunday in England - - - - - 151

CHAPTER XI.

Eating and Drinking.—Cookery.—Toasts.—Beer.—Tobacco - - - - - - 160

CHAPTER XII.

Love of Sports.—Fighting and Wrestling.—Fox-hunting - - - - - - 179

CHAPTER XIII.

The Drama and the Stage - - - - 187

CHAPTER XIV.

Literature. — The Fine Arts. — The Royal Society - - - - - - - 195

CHAPTER XV.

'The greatest Beauties in the World' - - 206

FOREIGN VISITORS IN ENGLAND.

CHAPTER I.

Introductory.—Royal Visitors.—Foreign Embassies.—Account of Cosmo, Prince of Tuscany, and his Visit to Charles II.

O see oursels as others see us' may be of as much service to nations as to individuals. The observer who sits down to record his impressions of a country which he is newly visiting, or even of one in which he has long dwelt, will make a high average of mistakes, due to the personal equation. The editor of M. TAINE's 'Notes on England,' granting that no foreigner has written more acutely and

instructively about England and the English than he has done, rightly judges that TAINE has not forgotten he is a Frenchman: that he has not mastered and never can master the true view of English motives and modes of thought and action.

Yet the foreigner, whatever his prejudices, is almost certain to contribute some new and startling points of view in which national characteristics may be presented. And it is not only in the department of morals that fresh knowledge of ourselves is to be thus acquired: it is surprising how very many unknown and unsuspected manners, and arts, and habits exist among us, concerning which we might remain for ever ignorant, were it not for the candid revelations of the intelligent foreigner.

The visitors to England, of whom we have records concerning their residence in this country, and concerning their observations on the strange and arrogant islanders, may be divided into three classes: as royal personages, ambassadors, and learned curious persons bent on the same ingenious inquiries to which our own adventurous countrymen have sometimes devoted themselves. And it must in justice be remarked that it is not always the most copious journal or diary which has furnished the soundest reflections: often the most meagre record has proceeded from the shrewdest head. It is quite vexing, indeed, in some cases, to note how little justice has been done to the opportunity, as, specially, in that of Marshal BASSOMPIERRE, who came as envoy to Charles I. from the Court of France; while others, men of quite ordinary faculties, have considered themselves bound, like MISSON, to say something about everything; or, like SORBIERE, have rendered themselves a laughing-stock, through their ridiculous assumptions and their habitual self-assertion. Some travellers, again, are easily imposed upon with fables by the current wag; while others, oppressed by the weight of their own prejudices, leave a fixed impression on the mind of their readers that an insular people is not the only intolerant one.

The arrival at Dover, or at Harwich, of a royal visitor to England has always been signalized by an affectation of unbounded hospitality. His own splendid equipage was paralleled by that of his host. Charles V., coming to England on a visit to Henry VIII., is said to have been accompanied by a retinue amounting in number to two thousand persons; Henry, not to be outdone in display, to which he was partial enough on his own account, went to Dover in person to meet the Emperor, with a numerous suite of knights and gentlemen. On these occasions the nobility and gentry residing on or near the route would join the escort, until relieved in turn by the magnates of the next county or district. And these attentions would sometimes be heightened in value by amusement being provided on the way, the thick woods of Essex and Kent furnishing ample means of sport. Even when the distinguished stranger was professedly *incognito*, as was COSMO, Prince of Tuscany, who came to England during the reign of Charles II., these courtesies were observed. There were few things, indeed, more pleasing to this prince's vanity than the continued attentions he received in this way; and, seeing that his progress to London began in Devonshire, it is not surprising that he reached the metropolis in a highly-flattered mood.

Sometimes the warmth of a royal reception would become more general, descending to the middle and lower ranks of society. When Marie de Medicis came to visit Charles I. and his Queen, the acclamations of the people were accounted 'extraordinary.' At Harwich and Colchester fireworks and music kept the rejoicings going till far into the night. According to the chronicler in the Queen's train, 'those of the most melancholy disposition changed their humour, in order to join in the general rejoicing.' At Chelmsford, 'all the neighbouring peasants, men and women, being assembled in different companies on the road by which her Majesty was to pass, without any other order or command than that which their own zeal had that morning imposed on them; some led by a violin, others by a bagpipe, all together received the Queen, dancing to the sound of these instruments, enlivened by a thousand acclamations of joy.' As for the Corporation of London, whether it was a friendly compliment to King Charles or not, they told the Queen-mother that the news of her arrival in the kingdom had struck them 'dumb with joy and admiration.'

The Embassy of the Middle Ages was usually an affair of splendour, with its following of knights, monks, and musicians; while the reception of an ambassador who was in any degree welcome was not much inferior in distinction to that accorded to royalty itself. Henry VIII., a 'King barbaric' in more senses than one, loved this sort of pomp, and lavished the most profuse attentions on every well-accredited visitor. GIUSTINIAN, Venetian ambassador to his Court, was met on the way to London by a company of knights, which being joined by the merchants and other Venetians then resident in London, made a stately escort of more than two hundred horse. The Court reception was exhaustive in its display alike of jewellery and of compliments. At the entertainments that followed, the visitors had the place of honour; and no pains were spared, so their eyes were dazzled and their hearts won by all that hospitality could suggest.

The particulars of this Venetian embassy to Henry VIII., due to the intelligent industry of the late Mr. Rawdon Brown, are among the most valuable items which modern research has furnished as lights upon the historic past. Mr. Brown having spent the best years of his life in residence at Venice, transcribing from the archives of that city everything bearing upon the diplomatic relations between England and the Republic, lighted upon these despatches and journals, and soon found that they might be made available for the general reader. There will be found, besides these of Giustinian, many curious shorter narratives brightening the pages of the calendars of State papers prepared by Mr. Rawdon Brown.

James I. was another complete master of the arts needful for the due reception of an acceptable embassy. Queen Elizabeth had always aimed at receiving her visitors in a manner worthy of her dignity; and during her long and brilliant reign numerous occasions arose for the exercise of hospitality and courtesy to distinguished strangers. Under her successor, such had been the progress of taste and order in these matters that an officer was appointed, in whose hands lay the proper reception of princes and ambassadors on their setting foot on English soil. Nothing could exceed the dignified cordiality of King James I. when he was in the mood to give an impressive welcome to a visitor. For proof of this the reader may be referred to Mr. Rye's 'England as seen by Foreigners in the days of Elizabeth and James the First.'

There is one well-known record of an embassy to the Court of Charles I., which is, however, excessively meagre: a circumstance much to be regretted, seeing how very shrewd are the observations which the writer did make. This was the renowned Marshal de BASSOMPIERRE, a man whose life was spent mostly among courts and fine ladies, when he was not on the battle-field. The world is absolutely a loser, in that BASSOMPIERRE was not such a gossip as SULLY, seeing that the class of people he met with were the courtiers of the early part of Charles's reign.

After the Restoration there was more freedom, more spontaneity, and less ceremony in English social life; especially in the Court of Charles II. Of this we have ample evidence in the 'Travels of COSMO III., Prince of Tuscany.' This, indeed, is one of the best records we have of the impressions formed by a foreigner in England at that period. A short review of this book will prove its manifest value to the historian.

The party landed at Plymouth at the end of March, 1669. They appear to have been expected, for some preparations had been made to welcome them. All the gentry in the neighbourhood, with the tradesmen of any note, received them with enthusiasm; while the populace, 'for want of room in the public streets, had filled the roofs of the houses.' COSMO was one of the last of the Medici family who acquired any distinction; and though now an almost forgotten name, was at that period possessed of sufficient reputation to deserve considerable attention as a visitor to King Charles II. His progress to London was a series of triumphs, in spite of his wish to preserve an *incognito*. At Exeter, being lodged at the New Inn, several gentlemen 'arrived from the neighbouring places to pay their compliments to him. Soon after, the Mayor, Aldermen, and bailiffs unexpectedly arrived in their magnificent habits of ceremony, with the insignia of justice and mace-bearers before them; they found his Highness upstairs in the saloon, who after having received them graciously, and desired the Mayor to be covered, heard and replied to their congratulations. He requested his Highness to be allowed to give him a public entertainment at his own house, which invitation his Highness refused, on the plea of his being *incog.*, and above all on account of the haste in which he was from his impatience to be in London and kiss the hands of his Majesty the King.'

They visit the cathedrals of Exeter and Salisbury in a spirit of reverence, tempered with regrets that orthodoxy has lost hold upon these once hallowed, but now desecrated, buildings. They must needs turn aside to Wilton, at Lord Pembroke's invitation. At Basingstoke they meet a troop of horse belonging to the Earl of Oxford, sent by the King as an escort. They reach London on the 15th April, and are lodged in the house of Lord Henry Germain, chamberlain to the Queen-mother. Introduced to the King at Whitehall, Charles welcomes his Excellency 'with a most courteous embrace, a reception demonstrative of cordiality and especial regard, and not common to all persons of quality, but reserved only for great and allied princes, others being only permitted to kiss his hand.' This incident is noted by Pepys (10th April, 1669).

Of Cosmo's residence in London, several notes may be taken concerning affairs which have long since passed from memory. St. Paul's Cathedral is still in ruins: 'Of this stupendous fabric there is nothing now to contemplate except the vestiges of its ancient magnificence, as only the principal walls (which mark the extensiveness of the building) are standing, together with the remains of the roof, of the larger nave, and of the pilasters which support it, and which separated the larger nave from the smaller ones, which latter yielded to the violence of the fire; and one sees only a huge heap of stones, cemented together by the lead with which the church was covered; this, when melted, fell among the ruins, which have entirely covered the relics of antiquity that were there formerly, and demolished many splendid monuments, both of Catholic bishops and other distinguished men, of which scarcely any trace is to be seen.' At Westminster Abbey they are struck with admiration at

Foreign Visitors in England. 13

the vaulted roof, and with reverence at the coronation stone, 'being according to tradition the same on which Jacob slept when he had in a dream the vision of the ladder, on which the angels ascended and descended.'

They attend a meeting of the Royal Society, and are much struck with the dignified and polite behaviour of the members present. The cabinet, under the care of Dr. Robert Hook, is 'full of the greatest rarities, brought from the most distant parts; such as quadrupeds, birds, fishes, serpents, insects, shells, feathers, seeds, minerals, and many petrifactions, mummies, and gums. . . . Among these curiosities, the most remarkable are an ostrich whose young were always born alive; an herb which grew in the stomach of a thrush; and the skin of a Moor, tanned, with the beard and hair white. But more worthy of observation than all the rest is a clock, whose movements are derived from the vicinity of a loadstone, and it is so adjusted as to discover the distance of countries, at sea, by the longitude.'

An account is given of a call made upon the Hon. Robert Boyle, which we cannot but regard as of intense interest. Himself distinguished for his literary taste, and his almost passionate search after useful knowledge, Count Magalotti waxeth enthusiastic over Boyle, 'whose works have procured him' (he says) 'the reputation of being one of the brightest geniuses in England. . . . This gentleman not only reduced to practice his observations on natural philosophy, in the clearest and most methodical manner, rejecting the assistance of scholastic disputations and controversies, and satisfying curiosity with physical experiments; but, prompted by his natural goodness, and his anxiety to communicate to nations, the most remote and idolatrous, the information necessary to the knowledge of God, caused translations of the Bible into the Oriental languages to be printed and circulated, in order to make them acquainted with the Scriptures; and has endeavoured still further to lead the most rude and vicious to moral perfection, by various works which he has himself composed. Indeed, if in his person the true belief had been united with the correctness of a moral life, nothing would have remained to be desired; but this philosopher, having been born and brought up in heresy, is necessarily ignorant of the principles of the true religion, knowing the Roman Catholic Church only by the controversial books of the Anglican sect, of which he is a most strenuous defender, and a most constant follower; his blindness, therefore, on this subject, is no way compatible with his great erudition. He showed his Highness, with an ingenious pneumatic instrument invented by himself, and brought to perfection by Christian Huygens of Zuylichem, many beautiful experiments to discover the effect of the rarefaction and compression of the air upon bodies, by observing what took place with animals when exposed to it; and hence may be learned the cause of rheumatisms, catarrhs, and other contagious disorders produced by air, and of various natural indispositions. It was curious to see an experiment on the change of colours: two clear waters, on being poured into one another, becoming red, and by the addition of another red, becoming clear again; and the experiment of an animal shut up in a vacuum, and the whole exposed to the pressure of the air. There was an instrument which shows of itself the changes of the air which take place in the twenty-four hours, of wind, rain, cold and heat, by means of a watch; a thermometer, a mariner's compass, and a small sail like that of a windmill, which sets an hand in motion that makes marks with a pencil as it goes round. There was also another instrument of a most curious construction, by means of which a person who has never learned may draw any object whatever. He showed also to his Highness, amongst other curiosities, certain lenses of a single glass, worked facet-wise, which multiplied objects; a globe of the moon of a peculiar construction, and several other things worthy of attention.' The Prince of Tuscany was so highly entertained with Boyle's experiments and curios, that he repeated his visit. The waterworks near Somerset House, and the rival machine at Vauxhall, invented by the Marquis of Worcester, came in for a share of his astonishment and admiration. The Guildhall had

Foreign Visitors in England. 17

'nothing remarkable' in it; but the India House, with its museum, gratified the party exceedingly. A visit to the House of Parliament, and to the principal courts of law, gives occasion for long disquisition by the Secretary on the constitution and laws, and the modes of dispensing justice. They have a jaunt to Chatham and Sheerness, and inspect the *Royal Sovereign*. Several days are occupied by a country excursion by way of Epping to Newmarket. The gaieties there are interrupted by an opportunity of seeing Charles touch for the king's evil, a matter which he always attended to on Fridays, 'according to the ancient usage of the first Catholic Kings of England, which was handed down to their successors, continued after the apostasy, and preserved to the time of the present King. . . .'

Passing through Cambridge, Northampton, and Oxford, Cosmo is received by the authorities with unbounded respect, the heads of the universities according him ovations in Latin; which the party cannot, however, follow, because of the strangeness of the

English pronunciation. Having rested at Billingsbere, at that time a seat of the Neville family, they pass through Windsor on their return. The Order of the Garter is a highly attractive subject. As they linger in St. George's Chapel, the assiduous inquiries of the Secretary result in his learning that the knights are 'obliged always to wear a garter of blue ribbon round the left leg, and are expressly forbidden to go out into public without this badge under a penalty of two crowns, which is the perquisite of the officer of the order who denounces them.'

The Secretary is much taken with King Charles. His cordial disposition, and his excessive politeness toward the Italians, count for much. But his Majesty's dabblings in science, and his devotion to 'the study of mechanics, mathematics, natural history, and chemistry,' appear to give him a still higher title to esteem. His pleasure-seeking is condoned throughout, and Cosmo's party are nothing loth to follow the merry

Foreign Visitors in England.

King to sport when opportunity comes in the way. Some of their most joyous days were spent at Newmarket, where coursing was going on, alternately with horse-racing, fowling, and the tennis-court. The struggles of these high personages to outdo one another in politeness are sometimes very amusing. The Duke of York at Court was as amiable as his brother. On one occasion the Duke called upon his Highness of Tuscany, who came downstairs to receive him. . . . 'On departing, the Duke wished not to allow the prince to go beyond the door of the drawing-room, but his Highness, not permitting so polite an indulgence, observed the same ceremony in descending the stairs as he had done in ascending, and accompanied his Royal Highness out of the door of the house, and remained there, though the Duke was very repugnant to it, till the carriage drove off.' Again: 'His Highness afterwards went to visit some ladies, that he might not be deficient in manifesting the same politeness toward them which he had shown to others, whose husbands had been to pay their respects to him.' On occasion of a banquet given by the Earl of Devonshire, the Prince 'walked from the top of the table to the bottom that he might gratify the guests, by giving them an opportunity of drinking toasts to his prosperity and welfare.' . . . Nor was any politeness omitted on the part of the Earl, 'who, for his knowledge, his manners, and his virtues, may justly be pronounced one of the politest and most accomplished noblemen in England.' His Highness, having spent a day at Hampton Court, examining the palace and grounds, and seeing a deer-hunt, pays his compliments to the King at Whitehall, in the evening; extolling, meanwhile, the glories of Hampton. His Majesty replies 'that the affection which his Highness entertained for the things of this country made him regard it with partiality; but that they could not be compared or put in competition with those of Italy.'

There are numerous odd illustrations of etiquette in small matters. On visiting the royal yacht at Sheerness, the Grand Duke was greeted with a salute from the guns as he sat

Foreign Visitors in England. 21

down to table; and every time his Highness drank, the discharge of cannon was repeated.

The Lord Mayor and Aldermen paid their respects to him one afternoon in order to request him to attend a feast in his honour: 'They had been received in form in one of the lower rooms by Colonel G——, who, to make the delay less tedious, had accommodated himself to the national taste, by ordering liquor, and amusing them with drinking toasts, till it was announced that his Highness was ready to give them audience.' The feast for the Corporation had to be relinquished, because of the Prince's *incognito* not permitting what would be in reality a State occasion. COSMO did not, however, omit what festivities lay within his reach; and the whole Court seems to have striven, one after the other, to induce him to honour their houses by accepting an invitation to dinner. The Duke of Buckingham, for example, gave a grand feast one evening, at which the King and the Duke of York were present. 'Toasts were not forgotten, being considered an indispensable appendage to English entertainment. His Highness began by proposing the King and the royal family, which was three times followed up with loud cheers by all present. His Highness, to do honour to the toast, would have given it standing; but this his Majesty would not allow, absolutely compelling him to keep his seat. In return for the triple compliment, the King pledged his Highness and the serene House of Tuscany in an equal number of rounds, and at the same time accompanied this act of kindness by taking hold of his Highness's hand, which he would have kissed, but the Prince, anticipating him, with the greatest promptitude and address kissed that of his Majesty. The King, repeating his toast, wished to show the same courtesy to his Highness; but he, withdrawing his hand with the most delicate respect, would not permit it, which his Majesty perceiving, immediately kissed him on the face. . . . The toasts given by his Majesty and his Highness having been thus mutually acknowledged and replied to, a concluding one was proposed, and drank with unbounded applause by the guests, to the intimate union and alliance of the royal House of England and the most serene House of Tuscany.'

These struggles between Charles and his visitor lasted to the bitter end. The Prince received his Majesty at supper on the evening before his departure. At the upper end of the table 'was placed on a carpet a splendid armchair, and in front of it, by themselves, a knife and fork, tastefully disposed, for his Majesty; but he ordered the chair to be removed, and a stool without a back, according to the custom of the country, and in all respects similar to those of the rest of the company, to be put in its place.' . . . After many toasts the entertainment was protracted to a late hour. The King at length took his departure, and when 'the carriage was about to drive off, the King's Majesty entreated the Prince to rest as soon as possible, on account of the fatigue which he would have to undergo on the following day, which was fixed for his departure; but his Highness, keeping his hand upon the door of the carriage to prevent its being closed, instead of taking leave, with great address stepped himself into the carriage to wait on his Majesty to the palace, in spite of the opposition of the latter. On alighting, his Highness repeated the politeness of offering his arm to his Majesty, who, however, would by no means accept of it. They went up to the King's apartments, where his Majesty and his Highness renewed their mutual compliments,' etc.

The Prince of Tuscany left London early in June, to return to the Continent *viâ* Harwich. The party dined at Thorndon Hall with Lord Petre, and the Secretary takes the opportunity of saying something concerning the quality of our cookery. 'The table was served with as much elegance and skill as is usually met with at the tables of English noblemen, who do not in general keep French cooks: their tables, in consequence, though distinguished by abundance, are deficient in quality, and in that exquisiteness of relish which renders the French dishes grateful to the palate. This is particularly the case with their pastry, which is grossly made with a great quantity of spices, and badly baked.'

He adds that there is also a great want of that neatness and gentility which is practised in Italy; for on the English tables 'there are no forks nor vessels to supply water for the hands, which are washed in a basin full of water that serves for all the company.' After resting for the night at the Black Boy inn at Chelmsford, they visit the aged General Monk, then residing at New Hall in Boreham, a dropsical invalid. Resting at Colchester, they go in the morning *viâ* Ipswich and the river Orwell to Harwich, whence they sail for Rotterdam on the 14th June.

CHAPTER II.

The Stranger's arrival in England. — French Manners.—English Treatment of Strangers.

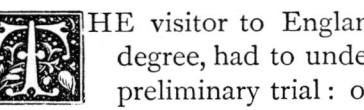HE visitor to England, of whatever degree, had to undergo one terrible preliminary trial: one from which no dignity, no pomp, no gold nor silver could deliver him. He must needs cross the Straits of Dover, and face the odious *mal de mer*. Most of our foreign friends tell the same sorrowful story: 'became so dreadfully ill that they thought they were dying,' or 'lay on the ship as if dead,' and so forth. There would be exceptions, of course. Queen Marie de Medicis, who had a fair trial of the waves, excited the admiration of her fellow-voyagers by her 'accustomed air and majesty.' That the Queen's immunity from sea-sickness was considered worthy of remark

Foreign Visitors in England. 27

is evidenced by the pen of the tender-hearted narrator of her journey: 'The Queen landed with an incredible joy, having been seven whole days in a continual storm; but certainly the compassion her Majesty had for her ladies and maids-of-honour gave rise to the greatest part of this satisfaction. And, not to speak falsely, the graces and attractions of these ladies were a little in disorder on their leaving the ship; for in so great and continued a storm they were more attentive to the alleviating their uneasiness than the preserving their beauty; everything about them seemed so sorrowful and so deplorable that the most beautiful among them touched the hearts of the beholders more with pity than with love; although after so many apprehensions of shipwreck the joy to see themselves safe in port possessed them so absolutely that one might observe, at the same time, the appearance of present joy and the marks of a past sorrow.'

Some travellers were willing to theorize on the subject of sea-sickness, but with no better success than later generations have done.

They found the passage of the Straits a grave interruption to the pleasure of their journey, and an inconvenience to which the highest and the lowest must needs submit. One of our own Kings, indeed, appointed an officer for his special assistance at sea. Hasted mentions the singular tenure of a manor in the parish of River, near Dover, which was granted to Solomon de Dovere, for 'the sergeantry and service of holding the King's head between Dover and Whitsond, as often as it should happen for him to pass the sea between those parts, and there should be occasion for it.'

The arrival at Dover, then, must have been commonly a pleasing change of circumstance. In spite of its proximity to France, Dover is, and probably always was, a peculiarly English town. There is a Kentish spirit in Dover not differing from that of the inland parts of the county; and, unless the recent years of quick and frequent intercourse have wrought a change, the town is singularly un-Frenchified for a place that has been thronged by passing foreigners for many centuries. So there is much novelty on the first arrival. One of the first discoveries made by a stranger is the delicious beer, 'most pleasaunte in tast, and holesomely relised,' which at once restores his appetite and revives his drooping spirits. The beer and ale of England are among the pleasantest surprises that lay in store for him.

But, whether from the visitor's own fault of manner, or because the brutal and the mischievous instincts were altogether irrepressible at sight of a foreigner, he had to run the gauntlet of the boys and the lower classes of Dover in a way that shocked his sensibilities. The experience of SORBIERE, who stayed in England during the reign of Charles II., is a fine example of this sort of annoyance, and of the affronts usually put upon the foreigner while in Dover. 'They fall,' he says, 'to the opprobrious term of *French dogs*, which is the epithet they give us in England—as I have heard them often call the French in Holland *mushrooms*, which yet is more tolerable than *Matto Francese*, *i.e.*, Foolish Frenchman, a name by which the common people of Italy are pleased to distinguish them. . . . To tell you the truth, both the one and the other make use of these opprobrious terms with some reason, upon account of the noise we make at our coming amongst them, and by way of reprehending a certain forwardness in us, which they call indiscretion, which in effect makes us appear very ridiculous to them. For this forwardness is so opposite to their serious temper, and the coolness of their proceedings, as well as to the patience with which they allow everyone to perform what he goes about. . . . These things depend so much upon men's behaviour,' etc. This gentleman presently gives a wise hint that some incivilities would be avoided by first acquiring a knowledge of the language. More than once his fellow-travellers 'not only declined in the inns to take care as they ought of a stranger, who could not tell how to make the people understand him, but I was as little regarded as if I had been a bale of goods. . . . I was desirous to show my civilities by my interpreter to those who were not so much tainted with rusticity, which they were so far from taking right, that they deemed it to be raillery, and an affront, which embarrassed me so that I must have recourse unto my interpreter to be duly apprised of it.'

There can be little doubt that people like SORBIERE suffered more of this kind of annoyance than they had need to incur. We do not find that less self-assertive persons make similar complaints. What they had to endure they endured in silence; and the reward of their self-respect was an early escape from the danger of being mobbed. Besides, the recollection of any too boisterous spirits on the part of the rabble of Dover sank into insignificance when a traveller found himself face to face with a London mob. Then he was indeed helpless. One can never know how many hundreds of lost and missing persons are to be put to the credit of the London rough— a race whose vitality has made his presence felt for centuries past, as of unexampled lawlessness and brutality.

SULLY tells the story of an incident which

placed him for a few days in a very delicate predicament. The first night of his arrival in London, some of his party got into a serious street brawl, which resulted in the death of an English citizen of respectable position in life. The populace, already prejudiced against the foreigners, as such, now began to threaten loudly, and followed the French to their lodgings with threats of immediate vengeance. . . . 'The affair soon began to appear of great consequence, for the number of people assembled was presently increased to upwards of three thousand, which obliged the French to fly for an asylum into the house of the ambassador. . . . The honour of my nation, my own in particular, and the interest of my negociation, were the first objects that presented themselves to my mind. I was also most sensibly grieved that my entry into London should be marked at the beginning with so fatal an accident. . . .' The culprit in the Duke's retinue was presently found to be a 'young man, son of the Sieur de Combaut, principal examiner in Chancery, very rich, and a kinsman likewise of Beaumont's [the

ambassador in residence], who, entering that moment, desired me to give young Combaut into his hands, that he might endeavour to save him. . . . "I do not wonder," replied I to Beaumont with an air of authority and indignation, "that the English and you are at variance, if you are capable of preferring the interest of yourself and your relations to that of the King and the public; but the service of the King my master, and the safety of so many gentlemen of good families, shall not suffer for such an imprudent stripling as this."
. . . . I told Beaumont in plain terms, that Combaut should be beheaded in a few minutes,—to be short, I desired Beaumont to quit my apartment, for I thought it would be improper to have him present in the council which I intended to hold immediately, in order to pronounce sentence of death upon Combaut. In this council I made choice only of the oldest and wisest of my retinue; and the affair being presently determined, I sent Arnaud to inform the Mayor of London of it, and to desire him to have his officers ready the next day to conduct the culprit to

the place of execution, and to have the executioner there ready to receive him.' The Lord Mayor, seeing the steps which SULLY had already taken to obtain 'justice,' and, perhaps, having some shrewd notion that provocation begun in the streets was too familiar a thing to warrant the shedding of a stranger's blood after the heat of the fray was over, exhorted SULLY to modify the sentence. But the Duke was inexorable, and would not consent to revoke it. He, however, deferred so far as to hand Monsieur Combaut over to the Lord Mayor, and thus resign him to the justice and laws of the city. 'I accordingly sent Combaut to him, so that the whole proceeding became a private affair between the Mayor and Combaut, or rather Beaumont; who without much difficulty obtained this magistrate's consent to set Combaut at liberty, a favour which none could impute to me. On the contrary, I perceived both the French and English seemed to think that if the affair had been determined by me it would not have ended so well for Combaut; and the consequence of this to me, with respect to the

Foreign Visitors in England. 35

English and the French, was that the former began to love me, and the latter to fear me more.'

The Abbé LE BLANC, writing from England early in the eighteenth century, notices the universal ridicule which some classes of his fellow-countrymen incurred by their conduct among strangers. He points out, with much justice, that many of the French who leave their country to seek a fortune elsewhere are 'not the sort of people that can give an adventurous idea of their countrymen: and yet it is from these adventurers that the English in general form their judgment of the French;' and he remarks that the characteristic Frenchman of the comedies has much to do with forming the popular prejudice:—' People in general think all the French are like those wretched refugees, who, in the coffee-houses of London, excite compassion rather than contempt. It is after these originals that the comic authors paint our manners: in one of their plays a French *petit-maître* drops a bit of cheese in pulling his handkerchief out of his pocket. . . .' But this worthy gentleman, in his charity toward both nations, admits that the frequent wars between them must have kindled their reciprocal hatred, which rivalry and jealousy in trade have kept alive in times of peace. And he justly claims that it is the vulgar and ignorant alone who habitually insult the foreigner; whilst the civilities, on the other hand, which are exhibited by well-bred people, seemed to him to be heightened by some desire to atone for the insults offered by the populace. The Abbé gives a curious anecdote of a stage-manager who, having on one occasion to restore the pit to good humour, bethought him of presenting a scene in which the French manners, customs, and especially cookery, were held up to ridicule. The artifice was entirely successful. Yet, withal, the imitation of French fashion had long set in, especially in matters of dress. The few young blades of fortune who travelled on the Continent of Europe brought back notions which either were at once adopted by certain sections of society, or speedily degenerated into mere fopperies,—

we have one story of a son being disinherited for wearing a French bag-wig. But the exigencies of female curiosity, and love of dress, could set all other authority at defiance; and the Parisian standards of fashion have fairly stood their ground.

MISSON is brutally plain-spoken, of course, on these affectations. 'The use of patches' (he says) 'is not unknown to the French ladies; but she that wears them must be young and handsome. In England, young old, handsome, ugly, all are be-patched till they are Bed-rid. I have often counted fifteen patches or more upon the swarthy, wrinkled phiz of an old hag threescore-and-ten and upwards. Thus the Englishwomen refine upon our fashions.' Again: 'The play-house, Chocolate Houses, and the parks in spring, perfectly swarm with fops and beaux. Their whole business is to hunt after new fashions. . . . They are creatures compounded of a periwig and a coat laden with powder as white as a miller's, a face besmeared with snuff, and a few affected airs.' 'A Beau is the more remarkable in England, because, generally speaking, Englishmen dress in a plain, uniform manner.'

To return: The testimony is overwhelming that, for many centuries past, foreigners, and especially Frenchmen, went about in danger of insults from the populace. It has been alleged that Philip, the husband of Queen Mary, complained bitterly of the insolence which he had to endure, in common with all foreigners, from the English people, insomuch that he found it difficult to live in England at all. So much does this defective trait weigh upon the minds of our visitors, that they devote much time and thought to its probable cause. It is usually put down to 'national pride,' until they have spent much time among us. After knowing the English people more intimately, they discover that our national pride, on the part of persons of any cultivation, involves courtesy as one of its leading instincts, and the great divergence of opinion on the matter seems to point to accidental circumstances in each case. The Abbé LE BLANC,

Foreign Visitors in England. 39

for example, declares that a Frenchman is much better received in London than an Englishman in Paris; that politeness to strangers is one of those virtues which the English dispute the most with French people. . . . 'As it is not supposed that pleasure brought them hither, the people make it one, agreeable to deceive their expectations. Their curiosity is regarded as the effect of their esteem for the nation; and pains are taken to justify it. . . . They know that strangers come hither to see men, and each particular person does his endeavours to give the most advantageous notion of the whole body.' After an admission that the common people of London are rough and ill-bred, he adds: 'The great civilities done by well-bred people are perhaps heightened by a desire to atone for the insults the populace are always ready to offer us, and which our very dress will sometimes occasion. . . . Moreover, here, as everywhere else, some of the vulgar are to be found in every rank and condition of life. . . . There are some here who cannot bear the sight of a Frenchman with tranquillity.'

The scholar LEMNIUS, two hundred years before this worthy Frenchman, experienced 'incredible courtesy and friendliness' while in England. PAULUS GIOVIUS, also in the sixteenth century, says, on the contrary, that the English are 'commonly destitute of good breeding, and are despisers of foreigners, since they esteem him a wretched being, and but half a man, who may be born elsewhere than in Britain, and far more miserable him whose fate it should be to leave his breath and bones in a foreign land.' PERLIN, half a century later, makes this astounding summary of our character: 'It is to be noted that in this excellent kingdom there is no kind of order; the people are reprobates, and thorough enemies to good manners and letters, for they don't know whether they belong to God or the devil, which St. Paul has reprehended in many people, saying, "Be not transported with divers sorts of winds, but be constant and steady to your belief."'

The anti-Gallican spirit has been ascribed partly to yet another cause. Nothing disturbed the average good nature of the

Englishman in past times so easily as the immigration of a body of foreign workmen, or the usurpation on the part of an Italian or Spanish merchant of a well-established source of traffic. The calendars of State papers reveal many curious incidents, founded on the attempts to restrain such foreign intrusions. It was bad enough for Popish ambassadors to bring a train of idle priests and monks; but for Huguenot refugees to come and settle in London and the big towns, with the avowed object of pursuing their handicraft, and thus necessarily supplanting many of the native artisans, was touching the people to the quick. They will have none of it. In June, 1551, five or six hundred men wait upon the Lord Mayor, complaining of the great influx of strangers, whom they are determined to kill, throughout the realm, if they find no remedy. In order to pacify them, the Lord Mayor causes a census to be made: forty thousand besides women and children are enumerated, 'for the most part heretics fled out of other countries;' precautionary measures are taken by the Corporation, so as to prevent breaches of the peace. In November, 1583, the Mayor of Norwich certifies to 4,679 strangers residing within the city, being Dutch refugees and others. In October, 1582, a plan is presented to the Secretary of State for the employment of French refugees in the manufacture of cloth and the erection of a wool staple in London. The year 1626 witnessed several efforts to ameliorate the hard lot of foreign tradesmen, and enable them to exercise their handicraft without molestation. In 1635 there was great influx of Walloons with their families, which caused the authorities of Dover considerable perplexity. Those who came with money, which they expended in the town, were tolerably welcome; but it was necessary to make many of them 'repair to more inland towns.' Now, this sort of thing had been going on for many years, perhaps since the reign of Henry VII. It is not difficult, then, to trace one mighty source of ill-humour. Mons. GROSLEY devotes a long chapter to a consideration of these international jealousies. He says that the refugees, whether rich or poor, were all incessantly exclaiming against

France, against the Court, and against the Jesuits, who had exerted themselves so much during the reign of James II. to establish their authority at Court. 'A considerable number of these refugees, being reduced to beggary, and to all the servility and meanness which that humble state either authorizes or suggests, exhausted and tired out the charity of the English, who soon used themselves to consider these beggars as representatives of the whole French nation.'

An anecdote from JOREVIN will illustrate the facility with which it was possible to become embroiled with an offensive character, solely on the ground of different nationality. He is waiting at Holyhead, along with a large party of persons intending to go by the Irish packet. 'Among them was a young man who spoke a little French; he was a clockmaker, and had worked in the galleries of the Louvre in Paris; with whom, entering into some discussion touching the skill and valour of the English, he said he should not fear two Frenchmen. "It would not be," said I, in answer to him, "a man of your sort that could terrify me sword in hand;" when all of a sudden he drew his sword, crying out, "Defend yourself!" Whilst I learned to fence at Rome, there were several English with whom I practised, and whose faults I easily discovered; and, in fine, observing this young man assaulted me precipitately, by keeping always on the defensive, and considering his default, I retired a long way, which caused this young giddy-headed fellow to throw himself almost out of all kind of guard. He had a sword of the French fashion, long and slender, that would not cut, which is the ordinary way of using the sword in England. Stopping, then, all on a sudden, I gave him a thrust in the under part of the right arm, which made him cry out to me, in the presence of many persons, who prevented me from killing him in the rage I was then in at being attacked by such a young coxcomb. I broke his sword on a rock, after having disarmed him, and he was blamed by all for having attacked me without cause.'

This Monsieur JOREVIN wandered over a great deal of England, and found, usually, a

Foreign Visitors in England. 45

friendly reception everywhere. It is not easy to make out his quality. He is well-educated, but credulous; and it is likely that he was simply an inquiring traveller. He never failed to make himself at home with 'mine host;' and there is no reason to believe that he was often molested by insolent persons. So it is not surprising that he gives us a tolerably good character. Here is one other anecdote of his, relating to an incident which might have had unpleasant consequences for a person of less self-control:

'At Stowmarket, where I lodged, a young man, a friend of the people of the house, entertaining me with several pleasant discourses, asked me whence I came and of what country I was, he well knowing by my manner of speaking English that I was a stranger, and by my clothes that I was a Frenchman; at the same time expressing his astonishment at my travelling the country alone. After this discourse he went out and gave notice to several burghers of the town that I was at such an inn, and that it would not be improper to know on what design I came to

England, by a way not usually frequented by passengers. In short, a little after I had supped, he brought up into my chamber the parson of the parish and his curate, who gave me to understand they would be glad to speak to me, and to learn some news from me; after which the minister spoke to me in Latin, declaring that he came on the part of the townsmen, to know who I was, and what business brought me among them. . . . Having contented them, they told me they were jealous of the French in England, ever since the suspicion of their having set the city of London on fire, whereby it had been lately almost destroyed. It was, however, necessary to drink two or three pots of beer during our parley; for no kind of business is transacted in England without the intervention of pots of beer. This being finished, the minister gave me all the absolution I could desire, and early in the morning I set off,' etc.

CHAPTER III.

Inns and Innkeepers. — A Pedestrian Visit to England.

ISITORS usually come *viâ* Dover and Canterbury. Sittingbourne was not an uncommon halting-place for the night; and one of the itineraries speaks of a Scotchman who kept an inn there, a good fellow, who could speak a little Latin. COSMO's party speak highly of their entertainment at Rochester. At Gravesend, another visitor extols the 'Flushing,' whose host is another intelligent and not ill-educated man. HENTZNER, who landed at Rye, was well entertained there, as is the case, he proceeds, 'everywhere in this country.' There is some variety in the experiences of our travellers, but any comparison with the Continental

auberge is usually favourable to those of our own country. The flippant MISSON has his experience confined to London; he seems to have been always ready to sponge upon a friend for board and lodging, and recommends others to do the same, unless they 'take a room ready furnished at so much a week.' But Misson was not a traveller, but rather an alien resident in London.

POLLNITZ, on the contrary, usually found a pleasant and unexpected welcome. Perhaps it was his very good fortune; but he had certainly better manners than MISSON, and courtesy goes farther, in a tavern, in promoting one's own comfort than almost anywhere. He always had the best of attendance and accommodation. Yet he found the 'reckonings run high.' Monsieur GROSLEY, likewise, is much taken with our country inns. He says: 'The towns and villages upon the road [this is between Dover and London] have excellent inns, but somewhat dear; at these, an English lord is as well served as at his own house, and with a cleanliness much to be wished for in most of the best houses of France. The inn-

Foreign Visitors in England.

keeper makes his appearance only to do the honours of his table to the greatest personages, who often invite him to dine with them.' This gentleman tells a story of an innkeeper 'boycotted' for extortion: The Duc de Nivernois having stayed at Canterbury, on his way to London, the innkeeper charged him, for supper, for himself and small retinue, forty or fifty guineas, which the envoy paid. 'The indiscreet innkeeper boasted of this imposition; but the gentry of Canterbury and the county of Kent, who held their assembly at his house, advised the Duke to prosecute the man for extortion. The Duke having, in the most positive manner, refused to sue for any satisfaction, the gentry, in the name of the nation, took upon them to revenge his cause, which they did in the manner following. They entered into an engagement to hold their assembly no longer at that inn, but to remove to another house. This resolution and these motives having been promulged in the public papers, all the English gentlemen who happened to travel through Canterbury thought themselves bound in honour to accede to the agreement. The inn being thus deserted, the innkeeper was ruined in the course of six months, and turned out of his house, after having seen all his goods sold to satisfy his creditors, who had likewise entered into the combination against him.'

The writer of the journal of Cosmo's travels says much in praise of English taverns. But then, his party went to the very best of them; and, in probably every case, preparations were made beforehand for their reception.

The Abbé le blanc gives a characteristic anecdote of his experience at Northampton, at a period when party-spirit ran unusually high. Having met, on the way to London, with a peer of the realm who desired that they might continue their journey in company, he consented to go with him. But he had to pay dearly for the honour of his lordship's company. 'Here each party has its particular

Foreign Visitors in England. 51

inns, and if a member of Parliament is in the opposition to the Court, he is under a necessity of going to an inn of his party, or he is a lost man; for either they would believe he had turned coat, or they would turn it for him. My fellow-traveller was much better off than I; for, finding the wine bad, he had recourse to the beer; and the fowl proving hard, he revenged himself on the pudding, which was soft enough. But I, who am not seasoned to this gross food, and drink little or no beer, I who am neither of the party of Corruption nor Opposition, neither Whig nor Tory, what business had I in this wretched house? This is not all: I saw the moment when I thought that our innkeeper's hatred to the Ministry would give him a right to sit down with us. We were obliged, at least, to drink out of the same pot with him to his health, and to the healths of all those of the town of Northampton, who were enemies to Sir Robert Walpole (against whom I have not the least subject of complaint) and friends to our landlord, with whom you see I have no great reason to be in love. And what is still worse, I was under a necessity of listening to the reasoning of this zealous partisan of the Opposition. My travelling companion had the politeness to entertain him during the whole supper-time; for it was not the innkeeper that made court to my lord, but my lord to the innkeeper. This last exclaimed bitterly against the corruption of the Ministry, and the remissness of the Parliament. My lord used his utmost endeavours to excuse the conduct of his party to our political innkeeper, and to persuade him that they constantly did all that was possible to be done in the present circumstances. "No, my lord," replied he in a passion, "they do not," etc. . . . Thereupon he wished us good-night, and departed in great wrath. As soon as he was gone, "Sir," said my fellow-traveller, "you must not be surprised at all this. In this country we are obliged to manage all sorts of people, in order to keep up our credit in the county. This fellow, notwithstanding his appearance, is rich; and rude and brutal as he is, he passes for an honest man, and is taken notice of; he is of greater importance here than you can well imagine; his vote at elections constantly guides those of all his neighbours."'

The practice of 'mine host' drinking as a matter of course with his guest was the survival of a more intimate form of entertainment. We have a story, nearly a century earlier, from Monsieur JOREVIN, who, staying at the Stag Inn at Worcester, has to make himself thoroughly at home with the host's family. 'According to the custom of the country, the landladies sup with strangers and passengers, and if they have daughters they are also of the company, to entertain the guests at table with pleasant conceits, where they drink as much as the men. But what is to me the more disgusting in all this is, that when one drinks the health of any person in company, the custom of the country does not permit you to drink more than half the cup, which is filled up and presented to him or her whose health you have drunk. Moreover, the supper being finished, they set on the table half a dozen pipes, and a packet of tobacco for smoking, which is a general custom as well among women as men, who think that without tobacco one cannot live in England, because, say they, it dissipates the evil humours of the brain.'

The experiences of a pedestrian, at a period when it was taken for granted that the pedestrian traveller was either a beggar or a vagrant in search of mischief, are well told by the worthy Moritz, who devoted a part of his sojourn in England to a walking-tour. It would appear that any traveller who did not choose, or could not afford, the stage-coach or post-horses, was regarded with anything but favour by the inhabitants of country towns and villages. Dusty shoes and clothes argued the tramp; the tramp bewrayed the beggar, or something worse. It will be admitted, however, by those who have tried it, that there is still in our own days a class of tavern where you need not present yourself with a soiled appearance; only it is far rarer to be repulsed than before the period when it became the fashion to make on foot the grand tour of English countryside.

MORITZ, then, having determined to see the heart of England as it only can be seen in perfection, ventured forth, after taking the stage as far as Richmond. He knows our poets by heart, and carries a Milton in his pocket. But he is ill-prepared for the unexpected contumely to which he is exposed. Having taken the road toward Windsor, he asks a man if he is on the right road to Oxford. '"Yes," said he; "but you want a carriage to carry you thither." When I answered him that I intended walking it, he looked at me significantly, shook his head, and went into the house again.' Having presently stopped by the wayside to rest awhile, and read his Milton, he soon finds this relief disagreeable, 'for those who rode or drove past me stared at me with astonishment, and made many significant gestures, as if they thought my head deranged. So singular must it needs have appeared to them to see a man sitting along the side of a public road, and reading.' Reaching Eton, he enters the inn, and is disgusted to find that they consider him but a beggar: 'I was tired, and asked for a bedroom, where I might sleep. They showed me into one that much resembled a prison for malefactors. I requested that I might have a better room at night. On which, without any apology, they told me that they had no intention of lodging me, as they had no room for such guests; but that I might go back to Slough, where very probably I might get a night's lodging.' They, however, 'suffered him to pay like a gentleman' for his dinner and coffee. The view from Windsor Terrace made him forget, in a moment, the insults of waiters and tavern-keepers. But as soon as he descended into the town, his troubles came back; for, although the landlord was courteous, the maid betrayed by her rudeness how small were her anticipations that the travel-stained visitor was likely to be able to pay his way. He certainly paid her, on leaving in the morning, with that best of all coins, a smart retort. 'At the door stood the cross maid, who also accosted me with, "Pray remember the chamber-maid!" "Yes, yes," I said, "I shall long remember your most ill-mannered behaviour, and shameful incivility," and so I gave her nothing.'

This unexpected difficulty haunted the poor pedestrian during the remainder of his journey, although there were occasions when the welcome was all that could be desired. At Henley he did not apply to the better class of houses; whilst no others would take him in. Having reached Nettlebed, after nightfall, he had better fortune, and he was received without much hesitation; although 'they certainly did not take me for a person of consequence.' The next morning, however, having put on clean linen, and making his appearance in better trim, 'they did not, as they had the evening before, show me into the kitchen, but into the parlour. I was also now addressed by the most respectful term, *sir;* whereas the evening before I had been called only *master:* by this latter appellation, I believe, it is usual to address only farmers and quite common people.' Similar experiences chequered his otherwise pleasant journey as he passed through Oxford and Stratford-on-Avon into Derbyshire. He at length found out that the surest way to favour, in the second and third rate houses, was to call for beer and drink the landlord's health. At length, having reached Leicester on his return journey, MORITZ had had enough of pedestrianism, and took the stage-coach back to London.

CHAPTER IV.

Praises of Kent.—Canterbury and Thomas à Beckett.—To London by Water.—The River Thames.

THE road through Kent pleased everybody — excepting, perhaps, MISSON, who can only record that 'the Kentish agues are famous.' SORBIERE extols the county in almost extravagant terms: 'Kent appeared to me to be a very fine and fruitful county, especially in apples and cherries; and the trees, which are planted in rows everywhere, make as it were a continued train of gardens. The country mounts up into little hills, and the valleys are beautified with an eternal verdure; and the grass here seemed to me to be finer and of a better colour than in other places . . . . All the country is full of parks, which yield a delightful prospect, and where you may see large herds of deer, etc.' A still more glowing description is that of LA MOTRAYE, some fifty years later, who counts the corn and the fruit-trees, the pippins and cherries, the best in the world. The oxen are the largest and best. There is an agreeable variety of hop-gardens, meadows, orchards, and cornfields.

Canterbury, 'one of the most famous cities in England,' is the goal of many anticipations on the part of our visitors, especially when of the ecclesiastical order. Before the Reformation, the tomb of Beckett was alone sufficient to attract the footsteps of piety, although the gorgeous aspect of the shrine, loaded with the precious gifts of two centuries of devotees, charmed the most worldly of sightseers. Here is a description, as it existed in Henry the Seventh's reign: 'The magnificence of the tomb of St. Thomas the Martyr, Archbishop of Canterbury, is that which surpasses all belief. This, notwithstanding its great size, is entirely covered over with plates of pure gold; but the gold is scarcely visible from the variety of precious stones with which it is studded, such as sapphires, diamonds, rubies, balas-rubies and emeralds; and on every side that the eye turns, something more beautiful than the other appears. And these beauties of nature are enhanced by human skill, for the gold is carved and engraved in beautiful designs, both large and small, and agates, jaspers, and cornelians set in relievo—some of the cameos being of such a size that I do not dare to mention it; but everything is left far behind by a ruby, not larger than a man's thumb-nail, which is set to the right of the altar. The church is rather dark. . . yet I saw that ruby as well as if I had it in my hand; they say that it was the gift of a King of France.' The Venetian ambassador GIUSTINIAN, in the next reign, recorded his emotions at sight of this dazzling shrine in a similar breathless tone. But, alas! a very few years of the new King put another face on the matter; and new visitors lament over the scattered relics and the lost treasures which Henry 'caused to be removed' under the pretext that the people venerated as a saint a man who had no pretensions to that title, or 'for other bad purposes, arising out of the false opinions he has.'

HENTZNER saw Canterbury just before leaving England, toward the close of Elizabeth's reign, when the Beckett *cult* was dead and buried. His note is short and quaint, and shows unerringly the entire revolution of sentiment which has passed over the religious side of the nation : ' In the vestibule of the church, on the south side, stand the statues of three men armed, cut in stone, who slew Thomas Beckett, Archbishop of Canterbury, made a saint for this martyrdom.'

The glorious church itself, sad to relate, became an object of far inferior interest after the great pillage. The free-thinking SORBIERE can only tell you how many paces long it is, and how many broad. As for MISSON, his irreverence reaches an extreme over Canterbury Cathedral : ' They show you the tomb of several Kings of Kent, and, if I remember right, some drops of Thomas à Beckett's blood ; something of him they have I'm sure, but can't well call to mind what.' It has been left for quite modern days, with a revival of taste for the best specimens of Gothic architecture, to restore the pilgrimage to Canterbury.

The journey to London by water was of infrequent occurrence—in fact, it is not easy to find a description of one earlier than that of MORITZ in 1782. As a good-hearted man, who saw everything with a poet's eye, and, moreover, a friendly one, he appreciated everything in England that was not downright offensive. His whole journal is indulgent, even in the midst of the inevitable annoyances that beset a stranger's footsteps.

He is delighted with the Thames: 'The charming banks of the Elbe, which I so lately quitted, are as much surpassed by these shores as autumn is by spring. I see everywhere nothing but fertile and cultivated lands; and those living hedges which in England, more than in any other country, form the boundaries of the green cornfields, and give to the whole of the distant country the appearance of a large and majestic garden. . . . The prospect toward Gravesend is particularly beautiful. It is a clever little town, built on the side of a hill; about which there lie hill and dale, and meadows and arable land, intermixed with pleasure-grounds and country seats, all diversified in the most agreeable manner.' With a party of his fellow-voyagers from Hamburg, he lands by boat at what is very probably Greenhithe; and as they walk to Dartford, is still farther enchanted with the beauty of the country, the goodness of the roads, and the neat village houses. They proceed by postchaises to London. This expedient, he says, is adopted on account of the crowded state of the river; it sometimes required several days before a ship could finish her passage.

London Bridge is, among our earlier travellers, the finest in the world. It is usually ornamented with the heads of criminals fixed on pikes; HENTZNER counted more than thirty. The appearance of the river, with its numberless fleets below bridge, and the constant flitting to and fro of wherries, gives the first overpowering impression of the wealth and magnitude of London. We have undoubtedly lost much of the striking look of

Foreign Visitors in England. 65

the city, as beheld by a spectator before the bridges were multiplied; a loss replaced, however, by the formation and planting of embankments. But, in spite of the mud bank and the old-fashioned wharf, there was a picturesque aspect about waterside London which pleased the visitor. Monsieur GROSLEY lamented the want of quays, and saw in this the tendency of human industry to destroy or to conceal the best means of showing our metropolis to advantage.

It would appear that the swans, which were formerly much more numerous than now, frequented the river as low down as London; and that an 'immense number' were to be seen off Whitehall in HENTZNER's time. More than a century later, the swans still attract the notice of visitors. And reference to the swans generally involves an allusion to the severe penalties attending any wilful injury to the birds. GROSLEY on one occasion witnessed the infliction of a penalty not set down in the statutes: a boy having been in conflict with a swan whose nest he had attempted to violate, left part of his nose behind him.

The palaces, from Somerset House upwards, contributed largely to the attractions of the Thames. The gardens at Somerset House, at Whitehall, and at intervals all the way to Chelsea, were conserved in a style which has never been since excelled. The riverside was adorned with trees and plantations; and it is probable that Westminster and its neighbourhood had very much the appearance now presented by the banks of the Thames between Sion House and Richmond Bridge, only with a background of stately buildings. Moreover, there was considerably more animation on the river two or three centuries ago, when Londoners were dependent to a greater extent than now upon the means of water-carriage. A remark of M. MURALT, who could see nothing in London, next to the Park, more agreeable or commodious than the river, gives us a strangely unfamiliar notion of the utility and convenience of the Thames: 'What pleases me besides is the gentleness of its stream, and a thousand little boats that cover it, and pass from one end of the city to the other when people have business, or for pleasure when they have none. On these occasions there are sometimes great numbers of hautboys and violins, which render the amusements on the water extremely delightful.'

Not less an object of interest to every stranger was a visit to Greenwich. In the days when the royal palace existed, there were frequent receptions. GIUSTINIAN, HENTZNER, and others who had the privilege of appearing at Court, have given enthusiastic accounts of the pleasure they experienced in attending royalty at Greenwich. On the way thither, in HENTZNER'S time, was to be seen 'the ship of that noble pirate, Sir Francis Drake, in which he is said to have surrounded this globe of earth.' This famous ship, the *Golden Hind*, had for several years been located in the creek at Deptford, by order of the Queen; and was a favourite resort of Londoners on some occasions of festivity. Several of our visitors mention it. In 1592 the party with the Duke of Wirtemburg saw it at Chatham being repaired and refitted. In 1614 another traveller saw the ship nearly all destroyed. In fact, it remained at Deptford till it decayed and fell to pieces.

CHAPTER V.

The Tower of London.—The City: its Streets and Shops.—St. Paul's Cathedral.—Westminster Abbey.

THE Tower appears to have solemnized the minds of some of our friends. It was regarded formerly as a substantial defence to the city. 'Nowadays,' says MISSON, 'it is nothing at all; for though it might, indeed, incommode the city, he that were governor of it must expect to perish in it, after having spit a little of his fire, as Samson perish'd when he destroy'd the Philistines.' Though, however, it was nothing at all for purposes of defence, the Tower was one of the wonders of London. The jewelry and the regalia brought very many strangers. According to the earlier accounts, the treasures and valuable property deposited in the Tower were said to 'exceed the anciently famed wealth of Crœsus and Midas.' 'A vast quantity of gold and silver is treasured up here,' says NICANDER NUCIUS; and it is evident that fabulous stories were long afloat upon this point. There were two cannon of immense size, made of wood, which Henry VIII. took with him to strike terror into the enemy before Boulogne; and a monster hand-gun, made for the same monarch, which it required a very powerful man to lift from the ground, is perhaps the item which JOREVIN, a hundred years later, took for 'William the Conqueror's musket.' A visitor of Elizabeth's time mentions at the top of the armoury an 'unspeakable number of arrows, which is a sufficient proof that the English used such things in battle in former times.' Another, in the following century, informs us that the Tower of London takes up a great deal of room in the pocket-books of gentlemen that travel; 'there they show crowns and sceptres, axes and clubs, lions, leopards, and other terrible things.' According to the 'London

Foreign Visitors in England. 71

Guide' of Dr. COLSONI, you gave up your sword on entering the precincts, to the yeomen, unless you were 'homme de guerre.'

The Royal Exchange, with its contiguous shops, was the leading object of interest to the secular eye. It was for long the finest building in London. Cheapside was the most attractive street, until it found a rival in that part of the Strand near Somerset Palace. Under the Stuarts a new Exchange arose, on the site of Durham House (near the spot now occupied by Adam Street); and this locality drew the rank and fashion of the day for nearly a century. JOREVIN alludes to Cheapside as 'the handsomest street in London, enriched with many fountains.' There were some who found fault with the meanness of the architecture of the houses as they stood before the great fire. The houses as they are now (except where in recent years palatial stonework has replaced them) are those which were so greatly admired in the rebuilt city;

and it is likely that Cheapside presented a very grand appearance at the period of Jorevin's visit. Everything was so abundantly new and fresh. Misson remarks, 'Ever since the great fire the people of London have built in a manner polite enough. Before that time their houses were the scurviest things in the world, as appears very plainly from whole streets still remaining nothing but wood and plaster, and nasty little windows with but one little casement to open. The stories were low, and widened one over another all awry, and in appearance ready to fall. Now the houses are built with brick, with even fronts—without magnificence, indeed, or anything like it, but with symmetry and neatness enough.'

In older times the visitors appear to have noticed less of the architecture of the streets and more of the display in the shop-windows. To judge from the remarks of some, there was a profuse exhibition of gold and silver plate and ornaments in several parts of the city. It must be Cheapside of which Hentzner speaks when he says, 'the streets in this city are very handsome and clean; but that which is named from the goldsmiths who inhabit it surpasses all the rest; there is in it a gilt tower, with a fountain that plays. Near it on the farther side is a handsome house built by a goldsmith, and presented by him to the city. There are besides to be seen in this street, as in all others where there are goldsmiths' shops, all sorts of gold and silver vessels exposed to sale; as well as ancient and modern medals, in such quantities as must surprize a man the first time he sees and considers them.' TREVISANO (*temp.* Henry VII.) mentions 'one single street,' in which there are fifty-two goldsmiths' shops, 'so rich and full of silver vessels, great and small, that in all the shops in Milan, Rome, Venice, and Florence put together, I do not think there would be found so many of that magnificence that are to be seen in London.'

At a later period, it is still admitted that London has the finest shops of any city in the world. The aspect of the streets was pleasing and animated. Fountains and crosses had disappeared; but the houses were more stately, and the streets could be traversed with more comfort than in Continental cities, because of the raised pathway. The squares were not invariably admired, for most of our friends were accustomed to see in their own towns large open courts or quadrangles; and those in London were not rendered more beautiful by 'adorning them with gardens,' partly because the shrubs and grass-plats reminded the spectator of a churchyard. The lighting of the streets was also considered an advance beyond that in other cities. MORITZ tells an anecdote of some German prince (whose name he does not give) who was so surprised at the almost festive illumination of the streets of London by night, that he seriously believed it to have been particularly ordered on account of his arrival hither.

There was a good deal of dirt about the streets of London far into the eighteenth century. The paving with flag-stones was to be seen only in the new streets. The inequalities of the roadway were a constant source of discomfort, from the tossing motion endured by the riders in coaches, and the continual danger of being splashed by the mud. But the saddest complaint against London was the smoke. St. Paul's Cathedral very soon shewed the powerful effect of the smoke upon the beautiful stone with which it was built, those parts exposed to the rain retaining much of its whiteness. Fears were expressed by Monsieur GROSLEY that, sooner or later, the inhabitants of London would have to bid adieu to any hopes of seeing the sun at all. 'The vapours, fogs, and rains, with which the atmosphere of London is loaded, drag with them in their fall the heaviest particles of the smoke; this forms black rain, and produces all the ill effects that may justly be expected from it upon the clothes of those who are exposed to it. Their effect is the more certain and unavoidable, as it is a rule with the people of London not to use, or suffer foreigners to use, our umbrellas of taffeta or waxed silk. For this reason, London swarms with shops of scourers busied in scouring, repairing, and new-furbishing the clothes that are smoked in this manner. This scouring is perpetual. Even the buildings themselves feel the effects of the smoke, and nothing can prevent their being injured by it.' His complaint goes still further, even to the interior of houses: the books, the furniture, the works of art, all suffer from the penetrating qualities of London smoke.

A good proportion of our earlier visitors are ecclesiastics, and we find them almost as enthusiastic over St. Paul's Cathedral and Westminster Abbey as they are concerning the Royal palaces. We have several notices of old St. Paul's. JOREVIN saw it in ruins, with the portico and a part of the nave still standing. HENTZNER appears to have made a careful and pious examination of the building, and copied down some of the inscriptions; he also mentions the 'very fine organ which, at evening prayer, accompanied with other instruments, is delightful.'

Sir Christopher Wren's church is admired from other points of view. Its immense size, and its adaptability to a Protestant form of worship, recommend it. One sarcastic fellow considers it is 'capable of putting a stop to all the corruption of London, provided the efficacy of the sermons is answerable to the largeness of the building.' In GROSLEY'S time (1765) the cathedral had begun to feel the effects of exposure to London smoke. This does not hinder him from declaring that it is a building worthy the admiration of 'all nations in Europe.' GROSLEY made some observations which are repeated to this day, and will continue to be repeated until Englishmen take in hand, in real earnest, the completion and proper conservation of St. Paul's. He objects, also, to the absurd contributions levied upon the visitors. This gentleman was present on the anniversary in May, when the Corporation of the Sons of the Clergy held their festival.

Far deeper emotions were aroused in the breast of the visitor to Westminster Abbey, than were ever excited by St. Paul's. The latter never seemed to be fully consecrated. Even the building destroyed by the fire had a somewhat unholy history; so long desecrated by neglect and misuse. But a sentiment of reverence was always aroused at sight of the interior of the Abbey. VOLTAIRE, who had no love for ecclesiastical buildings, except from a historic or an artistic point of view, gives vent to an unusual display of feeling over the memorials of the past with which the Abbey is filled. 'Go into Westminster Abbey (he says), and you'll find that what raises the admiration of the spectator is not the mausoleums of the English kings, but the monuments which the gratitude of the nation has erected to perpetuate the memory of those illustrious men who contributed to its glory. We view their statues in that Abbey in the same manner as those of Sophocles, Plato, and other immortal personages were viewed in Athens; and I am persuaded that the bare sight of those glorious monuments has fired more than one breast, and been the occasion of their becoming great men. GROSLEY remarks upon the incessant crowds who come to contemplate them : 'I have seen herb-women holding a little book which gives an account of them ; I have seen milk-women getting them explained, and testifying not a stupid admiration, but a lively and most significant surprise. I have seen the vulgar weep at the sight of Shakespeare's beautiful and expressive statue, which recalled to their memory those scenes of that celebrated poet which had filled their souls with the most lively emotions.'

Mention is made as early as 1610 of a printed book of the monuments, sold by the vergers. There was, besides, an account of the monumental inscriptions in the Abbey and in St. Paul's, published at Frankfort in 1618, by ARITHMÆUS. HENTZNER transcribes some of the epitaphs in his journal. These things speak of a tendency to heroworship which, the farther back we go, seems to overpower any more devout sentiment. HENTZNER had not a word in praise of the glorious structure itself, and seems to regard it as but a great mausoleum. After the close of the seventeenth century the tone is altered. Although there is little taste for Gothic architecture, Westminster Abbey comes to be admired as much for itself as for its contents.

There was one object of interest here—nowadays almost forgotten—which seized upon the awe-struck imagination of everybody. Scarce any visitor to the Abbey fails to record, with a mysterious regard, that he was shewn *Jacob's pillow*. Monsieur JOREVIN refers to it with a degree of faith which does not betray a moment's hesitation: 'Jacob's stone, whereon he rested his head when he had the vision of the angels ascending and descending from heaven to earth on a long ladder. This stone is like marble, of a bluish colour; it may be about a foot and a half in breadth, and is enclosed in a chair, on which the kings of England are seated at their coronation; wherefore to do honour to strangers who come to see it, they cause them to sit down on it.' All the itineraries mention it circumstantially, in full belief in its genuineness. Even as late as '*De Leydsman den Vreemdelingen*' (1759), the monkish tale is repeated. VON POLLNITZ has one of his racy stories to tell about this mysterious stone. The irreverent German says that 'amongst the relics which are still preserved in this church, there is one which for its antiquity I believe has not its equal, it being the stone which served for Jacob's pillow when he dreamt of that mysterious ladder which reached up to heaven. This precious relique is very much neglected, and I cannot imagine how it came to be so abandoned by that pious King James II. The English would do well to make a present of it to the Republic of Venice, where this stone would quadrate exactly with the piece of Moses's rock in St. Mark's Church. The Cardinal Cienfuegos showed me a piece of it when I was last in Rome: he told me that he stole it in his return from Portugal, where he had been ambassador, when he came to London with a commission from the Emperor to King George I. He added that it was the only robbery he was ever guilty of in his life, and that he should have been exceeding scrupulous of committing it if this stone had been as much honoured in England as it deserved; but that finding it neglected and despised, he could not help filching a piece of it, which he was so fortunate as to strike off with a key at the very nick of time when the keeper of it happened to be looking another way. I told him that I did not think that he needed to have been so very scrupulous of this theft; that I was persuaded that if he had given the keeper a guinea at most, he might have had a much greater piece, and that perhaps for a trifle more he might have brought away the whole stone.'

CHAPTER VI.

St. James's Park.—The Royal Palaces.—Theobalds. Nonesuch —Richmond.—Windsor.—Greenwich.— Queen Elizabeth and her Court.

HE royal palaces vie with the national monuments in the interest attached to them by the earlier travellers. Some of their journals are occupied by receptions at Court; while others confine themselves to a description of the contents of the buildings. The gardens at Whitehall and at Somerset House, with their terraces and lawns reaching to the river-side, furnished with statues and classical ornaments in a taste long since dead, must have been a great attraction to the Thames, to judge from the enthusiastic description of JOREVIN and others. St. James's Park is an adjunct to Whitehall Palace. 'Its great beauty consists in bringing, as it were, the country into the city.' A story

is quoted, by more than one visitor, that Charles II. intended to ornament the park with extensive designs, and sent to Paris for a 'skilful person' for the purpose; but after the expert 'had taken a narrow view of the place, he found that its native beauty, country air, and deserts, had something greater in them than any thing he could contrive, and persuaded the King to let it alone.' Charles spent much of his time in St. James's Park, almost unattended, except by crowds of fashion that followed him. Before his time, there must have been a still more rural aspect about the park, since deer and other animals were kept there, and the aviary and fowl preserves were more extensive than they are now. Charles loved to while away his time here, toying with the birds; and there was, in consequence, a great following of fashion tending that way. The time for good company, according to MISSON, was at noon on fine days in winter, and late at night during the hot days of summer. Besides the canal there were other large ponds and basins of water. The grass-plats would be covered

Foreign Visitors in England. 85

with deer and cows; and when the walks were full of company, there were united in one prospect 'the crowd, the grandeur and magnificence of a wealthy and populous city, and the striking contrast of rural simplicity.' A later observer speaks of the cows being driven to the gate near Whitehall, in the evening, where they 'swill passengers with their milk, drawn from their udders on the spot, and served, with all the cleanliness peculiar to the English, in little mugs, at the rate of a penny a mug.'

We have several notices of the palaces which have disappeared. James I. keeps court at Theobalds, Elizabeth at Greenwich, Henry VIII. at Greenwich and Windsor, Wolsey at Hampton Court, the Stuarts at Whitehall. There is a sameness about the descriptions of the various royal entertainments; excepting that, as one generation succeeds another, there is a manifest process of evolution from the barbaric to the elegant, from the mere display of 'pearl and gold' to the wider magnificence in which these things are mingled with poetry, and wit, and the mental accomplishments of an age which began with the Court of Elizabeth, and progressed rapidly in refinement under the Stuarts. The gardens, also, become an especial object of interest to some visitors. HENTZNER and his patron appear to have made a tour of the palaces, beginning with Theobalds, and he has really more to say about the adjacent gardens and parks than about the interiors. Count MAGALOTTI's journal is a treasury of the principal English gardens existing in the days of Charles II.

HENTZNER describes the garden at Theobalds as 'encompassed with a ditch full of water, large enough for one to have the pleasure of going in a boat and rowing between the shrubs. There are great variety of trees and plants; labyrinths made with a great deal of labour; a jet d'eau, with basin of white marble; and columns, and pyramids of wood and other materials up and down the garden. After seeing these, we were led by the gardener into the summer-house, in the lower part of which, built semicircularly, are twelve Roman Emperors in white marble, and a table of touchstone; the upper part of it is set round with cisterns of lead, into which the water is conveyed through pipes, so that fish may be kept in them, and in summer-time they are convenient for bathing.' Nonesuch palace he describes as 'so encompassed with parks full of deer, delicious gardens, groves ornamented with trellis-work, cabinets of verdure, and walks embowered by trees, that it seems to be a place pitched upon by *pleasure* herself to dwell in along with *health*. . . . In the artificial gardens are many columns and pyramids of marble, two fountains that spout water one round the other like a pyramid, upon which are perched small birds that stream water out of their bills. In the grove of Diana is a very agreeable fountain, with Actæon turned into a stag, as he was sprinkled by the goddess and her nymphs; with inscriptions.' There is something of an artificiality of taste in all this; but HENTZNER does not fail to go into raptures over an aspect less dependent on the hand of man. Witness his notice of the view from Windsor Castle: 'The situation is entirely

Foreign Visitors in England.

worthy of being a royal residence; a more beautiful being scarce to be found. From the brow of a gentle rising, it enjoys the prospect of an even and green country; its front commands a valley extended every way, and chequered with arable lands and pasturage, clothed up and down with groves, and watered by that gentlest of rivers the Thames,' etc.

There are some references to Richmond Palace, bearing upon courtly entertainments there; but very little is said of the structure or its contents. More than one writer, however, alludes to King Henry VII's Chamber 'where he is said to have died, the wall of which is besprinkled with his blood.' Mention is made also of a 'large mirror, in which Henry was able to see what he wished; but this mirror broke in pieces of itself when the King died.'

Several of our visitors are tempted into long inventories of the contents of the royal palaces. There is one quoted by Mr. Rye, which occupies several pages. The following, from HENTZNER, will give a vivid idea of the dazzling curiosities which attracted the fancy, and were thought 'worthy of observation' in Whitehall:

'The royal library, well stored with Greek, Latin, Italian, and French books: among the rest, a little one in French, upon parchment, in the handwriting of the present reigning Queen Elizabeth. . . . All these books are bound in velvet of different colours, though chiefly red, with clasps of gold and silver; some have pearls and precious stones set in their bindings.

'Two little silver cabinets of exquisite work, in which the Queen keeps her paper, and which she uses for writing-boxes.

'The Queen's bed, ingeniously composed of woods of different colours, with quilts of silk, velvet, gold, silver, and embroidery.

'A little chest ornamented all over with pearls, in which the Queen keeps her bracelets, ear-rings, and other things of extraordinary value.

'Christ's Passion, in painted glass.

'Portraits: among which are, Queen Elizabeth at sixteen years old; Henry, Richard, Edward, Kings of England; Rosamond, etc.

'A small hermitage, half hid in a rock, finely carved in wood.

'Variety of emblems, on paper, cut in the shape of shields, with mottoes, used by the nobility at tilts and tournaments, hung up here for a memorial.

'Different instruments of music, upon one of which two persons may perform at the same time.

'A piece of clockwork, an Ethiop riding upon a rhinoceros, with four attendants, who all make their obeisance when it strikes the hour; these are all put into motion by winding up the machine.'

Among the curiosities at Windsor is a unicorn's horn, 'above eight spans and a half in length, valued at £10,000.' At Hampton Court everything is so gorgeous and costly, that the walls of the palace 'shine with gold and silver.' . . . 'Here is, besides, a certain cabinet called Paradise, where everything glitters so with silver, gold and jewels, as to dazzle one's eyes; and a musical instrument made all of glass, except the strings.'

The chapel at Windsor appears to have been celebrated for its music. GIUSTINIAN was enchanted with it. The visit of Frederick, Duke of WIRTEMBERG, is marked by expressions of great delight by the writer of his journal. 'In the church his Highness listened for more than an hour to the beautiful music, the usual ceremonies, and the English sermon. . . The music, especially the organ, was exquisitely played. . . . and there was likewise a little boy who sang so sweetly amongst it all, and threw such a charm over the music with his little tongue, that it was really wonderful to listen to him.' The reception of GRUTHUYSE, at Windsor, when he attended the Court of Edward IV., as described in an ancient manuscript of the period, is a highly-interesting illustration of life in Windsor Castle: The King prepares three chambers, richly hung with cloth of arras, for the use of his visitor; after having interviewed the King, the Lord Chamberlain conducts GRUTHUYSE to his chamber for supper. After supper the King requests his company, and accompanies him to the Queen's apartments, where she and her ladies are playing at ninepins and divers other games, besides dancing, 'the whiche sight was full plesaunte to them.' ... 'In the morninge, when Matyns was done, the King herde in his owne chappell our ladye masse, whiche was melodyousely songe, the Lorde Grautehuse being there presente.' After mass is over the King presents him with a golden cup, garnished with pearls, having inside a piece of a unicorn's horn, and on the outer cover a large sapphire. After breakfast the King has him and 'all his compeny into the lyttle parke, where he made hym to have greate sporte. And there the Kinge made hym ryde on his owen horse, on a right feyre hoby, the whiche the Kinge gave hym.' He also gave him 'a royall crosbowe, the strynge of silke, the case covered w^t velvette of the King's collours, and his arms and badges thereupon; also the heddes of quarrelles were gilte.' In the afternoon there was hunting; 'there were slaine halfe a doussein buckes, the whiche the Kinge gave to the sayde Lorde Grautehause. By that tyme it was nere night, yett the Kinge shewed hym his garden, and Vineyard of Pleasour, and so turned into the castell agayne, where they herde evensonge in theire chambers.' Then the Queen, another day, has a great banquet. 'Item, there was a syde table, at the whiche satte a greate vue of ladyes.' . . . 'And when they had soupped, my Lady Elizabeth, the Kinge's eldest doughter, daunsed with the Duke of Buckingeham, and divers other ladyes also. Then about ix. of the clocke, the Kinge and the Quene, w^t her ladyes and gentlewomen, brought the sayde Lorde Grautehouse to iij. chaumbres of pleasance, all hanged w^t whyte sylke and lynnen clothe, and all the floures covered w^t carpettes. There was ordeined a bedde for hymselve, of a good doune as coulde be gotten, the shetes of Raynys, [stuff from *Rennes*] also fyne fustyans; the counterpoynte clothe of golde, the curteyns of whyte sarsenette. . . . In the iij^{de} chambre was ordeined a bayne [bath] or ij, which were covered w^t tentes of whyte clothe.' Presently the Lord Chamberlain assists him to prepare for the bath. After they have bathed, they have 'grene gynger, divers cyryppes, comfyttes, and ipocras,' and then retire to bed.

A picture of the Court of Queen Elizabeth will form a powerful contrast to the above. When HENTZNER came, in 1598, the Queen was getting on in years, and her appearances in public were marked by sobriety and dignity. She generally dwelt at Greenwich. She was born in this palace, and spent most of her summers here after she came to the throne. To the very last she enjoyed the park and the river, and here she usually received her visitors. HENTZNER'S particularly vivid and graphic notice is one of the best accounts extant of Elizabeth in her old age :

'We were admitted into the presence-chamber, hung with rich tapestry, and the floor strewed with hay, after the English fashion, through which the Queen commonly passes in her way to chapel. At the door

Foreign Visitors in England.

stood a gentleman dressed in velvet, with a gold chain, whose office was to introduce to the Queen any person of distinction that came to wait upon her. It was Sunday, when there is usually the greatest attendance of nobility. In the same hall were the Archbishop of Canterbury, the Bishop of London, a great number of Councillors of State, Officers of the Crown, and gentlemen, who waited the Queen's coming out, which she did from her own apartment, when it was time to go to prayer, attended in the following manner: First went gentlemen, barons, earls, knights of the garter, all richly dressed, and bareheaded; next came the chancellor, bearing the seals in a red silk purse, between two—one of which carried the royal sceptre, the other the sword of state, in a red scabbard studded with golden fleur-de-lys, the point upward; next came the Queen (in the sixty-fifth year of her age, as we were told), very majestic; her face oblong, fair, but wrinkled; her eyes small, yet black and pleasant; her nose a little hooked, her lips narrow, and her teeth black; she had in her ears two pearls, with very rich drops; she wore false hair, and that red; upon her head she had a small crown, . . . her bosom was uncovered, as all the English ladies have it till they marry, and she had on a necklace of exceeding fine jewels; her hands were small, her fingers long, and her stature neither tall nor low; her air was stately, her manner of speaking mild and obliging. That day she was dressed in white silk, bordered with pearls of the size of beans, and over it a mantle of black silk, shot with silver threads; her train was very long, the end of it borne by a marchioness; instead of a chain she had an oblong collar of gold and jewels. As she went along in all this state and magnificence she spoke very graciously, first to one, then to another, whether foreign ministers or those who attended for different reasons, in English, French, and Italian; for, besides being well skilled in Greek, Latin, and the languages I have mentioned, she is mistress of Spanish, Scotch and Dutch. Whoever speaks to her it is kneeling, and now and then she raises some with her hand. While we were there W. Slawata, a Bohemian baron, had letters to present to her; and she, after pulling off her glove, gave him her right hand to kiss, sparkling with rings and jewels, a mark of particular favour. Whereon she turned her face as she was going along; everyone fell down on the knees. The ladies of the court followed next to her, very handsome and well-shaped, and for the most part dressed in white; she was guarded on each side by the gentlemen pensioners, fifty in number, with gilt battle-axes. In the antechapel, next the hall where we were, petitions were presented to her, and she received them most graciously, which occasioned the acclamation of "Long live Queen Elizabeth!" She answered it with, "I thank you, my good people!" In the chapel was excellent music. As soon as it and the service were over, which scarce exceeded half an hour, the Queen returned in the same state and order, and prepared to go to dinner.'

He then details the ceremonies attendant on the preparation of her dinner-table, and concludes:

'At last came an unmarried lady, and along with her a married one, bearing a tasting-knife; the former was dressed in white silk, who, when she had prostrated herself three times in the most graceful manner, approached the table, and rubbed the plates with bread and salt with as much awe as if the Queen had been present. When they had waited there a little while the Yeomen of the Guards entered, bareheaded, clothed in scarlet, with a golden rose upon their backs, bringing in at each turn four dishes, served in plate, most of it gilt; these dishes were received by a gentleman in the same order they were brought, and placed upon the table, while the lady-taster gave to each of the guard a mouthful to eat of the particular dish he had brought, for fear of any poison. During the time that this guard, which consists of the tallest and stoutest men that can be found in all England, being carefully selected for this service, were bringing dinner, twelve trumpets and two kettle-drums made the hall ring for half an hour together. At the end of all this ceremonial a number of unmarried ladies appeared, who, with particular solemnity, lifted the meat off the table, and conveyed it into the Queen's inner and more private chamber, where, after she had chosen for herself, the rest goes to the ladies of the court. The Queen dines and sups alone, with very few attendants; it is very seldom that anybody, foreigner or native, is admitted at that time, and then only at the intercession of somebody in power.'

CHAPTER VII.

Various Sovereigns of England.—The Houses of Parliament.—Political liberty of the English people.

T is noticeable that our visitors have usually spoken of the English Sovereigns with respect. One of them says : 'a monarch of England is capable of doing as much good as any king in the world, but he can do no wrong.' Perhaps this idea has pervaded the minds of some in a double sense, as though it were of no use to point out the faults of those who could not possibly offend. And yet, upon review of the persons who have occupied the English throne since the death of Henry VIII., it is difficult to point to one of them who has not earned some title to the affection of the people. Even Mary, before she became the tool of the Papists, and succumbed to the detestable in-

fluences of religious bigotry, was beloved and admired by all who knew her. As a rule, the average stranger's estimate of each one of them does not differ much from our own, after we have subtracted the enmities aroused by bigotry and partizanship. James I. is the pedantic wiseacre; generous, hospitable, princely, and amiable. Elizabeth is always the accomplished and dignified Queen, celebrated for her elegance, both of body and mind. Charles I. is the pink of courtesy and piety; and Charles II. 'beloved by all ranks, for his birth, for his virtues and his knowledge, and for the gentleness with which he treats his people.' MISSON'S summary of Charles II. is unique, and cannot be said to be altogether inaccurate: 'A good prince, a man of wit, curious in physical and mechanical experiments; a pensioner of France, a Roman Catholic, if anything; sick of being tossed from pillar to post, he was resolved to spend the latter part of his life in peace; fonder of women, ease, and pleasure, than of Dunkirk, England, and all the crowns in the universe.' As for James II., MISSON is willing to credit him with the qualities of a great prince, if he could but 'follow the light of reason, and the natural inclinations of his heart.' But allowing the Jesuits to beset him, in season and out of season, must needs bring misfortune upon him. 'Those cursed probabilities, equivocations, directions of the intentions, maxims of keeping no faith with heretics, and other the like principles invented by the enemy of God and man, possess'd his mind, fill'd him with fatal prejudices, and led him to be guilty of perjury with an honest and good intention.'

Mons. GROSLEY offers some just observations on the relation between the English monarch and his subjects, in the course of which he remarks how rare it is for men to love those who force their esteem, or to always esteem those whom they love. Henry VII. and William III., the wisest princes that ever reigned in England, he points to as belonging to the former category; while Charles II. (of course!) was 'greatly beloved, and little esteemed.' GROSLEY considers that if any king ever deserved the love of his subjects, it was the reigning sovereign. George III. had then been only five years on the throne; and the sobriety of his Court, and the simplicity of his mode of life, added to the constant affability of his manners, were a striking novelty in the records of monarchy. 'All those he speaks to he accosts in the most polite manner, and never opens his lips except to say the most obliging things.' His palace practically unguarded, and his 'country retreat inferior in magnificence to many'; together with the very much lessened state of his equipages, pointed to one means among many of acquiring popular esteem. Yet, our friendly visitor observes that coachmen and carmen never stop at his approach, and take a pride in not bowing to him. 'Why should we bow to George?' say the insolent rabble; 'he should bow to us. He lives at our expense!'

It is such a startling development of the principle of personal freedom, as this anecdote furnishes, which so frequently amazed the stranger on our shores. The objects to which deference was paid in his own country were not those specially adored by Englishmen; and, contrariwise, he found here often a bigoted adherence to principles which he had been accustomed to regard as harmless superstitions. Liberty he found to be a fetish, at the feet of which the whole nation professed unmixed devotion. Yet he often ended with the conclusion that it was a delusive worship. The English people appeared to enjoy unbridled license to speak and to write what they liked, and to settle their little differences by mob-authority. All men, as in most other civilized countries, were aspiring to a sort of equality; and in that all men were engaged in a perpetual warfare. 'They believe they enjoy liberty (says LE BLANC) because they have the *word* for a device; but those who find themselves invested with power, by feeding the rest with chimerical ideas find means to really enslave them.' This gentleman elsewhere sarcastically remarks that the very general study of politics here disorders more heads than it regulates, because it 'demands an application which the majority of mankind are not equal to, and such lights as but very few men have an opportunity of acquiring.' It is hinted, by more than one writer, that under such a free constitution as that of England there was no medium left between slavery and liberty. This is an extreme notion. But the tyranny of majorities, duped by fine-sounding names, and led off by plausible language, doubtless appeared to such minds to foreshadow a peril to which the English nation must necessarily be exposed. Mons. Louis SIMOND, a later writer, is extremely puzzled because he finds that there is already a very general personal liberty in England for all persons, whether enfranchised or not. He observes that the right of making laws does not in itself constitute liberty; and he quotes (though not with entire approval) a sarcasm of Rousseau's: 'The English think they are free, but they are much mistaken. They are so only during an election of members of parliament; as soon as this election is made, they are slaves, they are nothing; and the use they make of their liberty during the few moments of its duration shows how little they deserve to keep it.'

Mons. GROSLEY holds that, as factions exist in both Houses of Parliament, an excellent means of bringing them together and uniting them on great principles is provided in the very contest aroused. 'Like those ebullitions of humour to which man is exposed in proportion to the strength and vigour of his constitution, these factions are at once the symptoms and the effects of real strength in any State.' GROSLEY appears to have acquired, in taking this point of view, a very just notion of the causes which have combined, on the one hand to enable the English Constitution to disencumber itself from time to time of corruptive elements, and on the other to avert the consequences of revolutionary passion. And it was doubtless with similar reflections that many of the constitution-mongers of 1789 indulged themselves with hopes of copying, in some of its essentials, a system which had worked so well. The intelligent foreigner of the present century devotes less attention to abstract than to concrete questions. We hear, therefore, less of comment on constitutional maxims than of the look of things. A visit to the Houses of Parliament is one of the sights they come to London for. But they are, as a rule, more interested in methods of procedure, in petty ceremonies. Americans especially take note of the circumstance that pens, ink and paper are not supplied to individual members of Parliament, and of the personal appearance of the speakers of renown. We hear how they are squeezed in the strangers' gallery; and the result of an application for an interview with a member in the lobby. The House of Commons is 'gorgeous,' and the House of Lords 'blazes in crimson and gold.' As for the occupiers of the benches, 'are they gods or men? They are truly but men; and they are men who all wear their hats on as at a Quaker meeting. But it is no Quaker meeting; for the spirit of heavenly repose which broods over the assemblies of the saints is surely not here,' etc.

We have, however, some few personal references which deserve to be noticed. The Prince PÜCKLER-MUSKAU, whose Tour is a delightful repository of anecdote of character, tells us how he endured six hours of heat and discomfort for the sake of seeing the House of Commons at its best. He was present at a debate during the ministerial crisis in 1827. He describes the clear torrent of Brougham's eloquence, now torturing with sarcasm, now taking a higher flight, working upon the sensibilities or convincing the reason of his hearers, riveting the attention without once pausing or halting, without repeating or recalling or mistaking a word. Yet with all his pungent wit and rare presence of mind, he felt that Brougham possessed the power of touching the heart in a far lower degree than his immediate opponent, Canning. 'If his predecessor might be compared to a dexterous and elegant boxer, Canning presented the image of a finished antique gladiator. All was noble, refined, simple; then suddenly, at one splendid point, his eloquence burst forth like lightning, grand

and all-subduing.' On an ensuing day, our visitor was in the Lords' House, and saw the Duke of Wellington : 'he is no orator, and was compelled *bon gré mal gré*, to enter upon his defence like an accused person. He was considerably agitated; and this senate of his country, though composed of men whom, individually, he perhaps did not care for, appeared more imposing to him *en masse* than Napoleon and his hundred thousands. There was something touching to me in seeing the hero of this century in so subdued a situation. He stammered much, interrupted and involved himself; but at length, with the help of his party, who at every stumbling-block gave him time to collect himself by means of noise and cheers, he brought the matter tolerably to a conclusion. He occasionally said strong things, probably stronger than he meant, for he was evidently not master of his stuff. Among other things, the following words pleased me exceedingly : "I am a soldier, and no orator. I am utterly deficient in the talents requisite to play a part in this great assembly. . . ." All the lords who had resigned made their apology in turn, as well as they could. Old Lord Eldon tried the effect of tears, which he always has at hand on great occasions; but I did not see that they produced any corresponding emotion in the audience. . . . Lord Holland distinguished himself as usual by sharp and striking exposition; Lord King by a great deal of wit, not always in the best taste; Lord Lansdowne by calm, appropriate statement, more remarkable for good sense than for brilliancy. Lord Grey far excelled the rest in dignity of manner, a thing which English orators, almost without exception, either neglect or cannot acquire.' This writer notices the extreme decorum visible in the House of Lords, as compared with the aspect of the Lower House, 'which is like a dirty coffee-house, and where many of the representatives of the people lie sprawling on the benches with their hats on, and talking of all sorts of trifles while their colleagues are speaking.' He owns to a mixture of impressions after having seen the collective wisdom in session, 'at once elevating and melancholy

—the former when I fancied myself an Englishman, the latter when I felt that I was a German. . . . This twofold Senate of the people of England' (he proceeds to say) 'spite of all the defects and blemishes common to human nature, which are blended in its composition, is yet something in the highest degree grand; and in contemplating its power and operation thus near at hand, one begins to understand why it is the English nation is, as yet, the first on the face of the earth.'

Professor SILLIMAN, from Boston, saw the House of Commons in 1805, and presents us with the aspect of Pitt and Fox toward the close of their careers. When the former rose to speak there was 'nothing in the subject which called for a display of eloquence; he made simply a statement of facts; but this served to identify his voice and manner. In his person he is tall and spare; he has small limbs, with large knees and feet; his features are sharp; his nose large, pointed, and turning up; his complexion sanguine; his voice deep-toned and commanding, yet sweet and perfectly well modulated; and his whole presence, notwithstanding the want of symmetry in his limbs, is, when he rises to speak, full of superiority and conscious dignity.' ... 'Fox's manner is flowing, easy, and natural, but without the dignity and impressiveness of Pitt. He stood leaning forward, as if going uphill, and his fists were clenched and thrust into his waistcoat-pockets,' etc.

Herr MORITZ tells us of Fox's appearance (1782) at an earlier period of his life, as a short, fat, and gross man, with a swarthy complexion, 'and, in general, badly dressed. There is certainly something Jewish in his looks. But, upon the whole, he is not an ill-made nor an ill-looking man, and there are many strong marks of sagacity and fire in his eyes.' Taking his place near the table, he gave it 'many a violent and hearty thump, either to aid or to show the energy with which he spoke. ... It is impossible for me to describe with what fire and persuasive eloquence he spoke; and how the Speaker in the chair incessantly nodded approbation from beneath his solemn wig. Innumerable voices incessantly called out, "Hear! hear!" and when there was the least sign that he intended to leave off speaking, they no less vociferously exclaimed, "Go on!" and so he continued to speak for nearly two hours.' Burke he describes as a well-made, tall, upright man, looking elderly and broken. Mr. Rigby is 'excessively corpulent, and he has a jolly rubicund face.'

This intelligent and good-natured German preferred the entertainment he met with at the Houses of Parliament 'to most other amusements.' Deeply impressed with the opportunity of seeing 'the whole of the British nation assembled in its representatives,' although in 'rather a mean-looking building, that not a little resembles a chapel,' he is yet naturally struck with some of the comic aspects of the business. 'The members of the House of Commons have nothing particular in their dress; they even come into the House in their great-coats, and with boots and spurs. It is not at all uncommon to see a member lying stretched out on one of the benches while others are debating. Some crack nuts, others eat oranges, or whatever else is in season. There is no end to their going in and out; and as often as any-one wishes to go out he places himself before the Speaker, and makes him his bow, as if, like a school-boy, he asked his tutor's per-mission. Those who speak seem to deliver themselves with but little, perhaps not always with even a decorous, gravity. . . . If it happens that a member rises who is but a bad speaker, or if what he says is generally deemed not sufficiently interesting, so much noise is made, and such bursts of laughter are raised, that the member who is speaking can scarcely distinguish his own words. This must needs be a distressing situation; and it seems then to be particularly laughable when the Speaker in his chair, like a tutor in a school, again and again endeavours to restore order.' . . . 'As all speeches are directed to the Speaker, the members always preface their speeches with *Sir;* and he, on being thus addressed, generally moves his hat a little, but immediately puts it on again.

This *sir* is often introduced in the course of their speeches, and serves to connect what is said; it seems also to stand a speaker in some stead when his memory fails him, or he is otherwise at a loss for matter. For while he is saying *sir*, and has thus obtained a little pause, he recollects what is to follow.'
. . . 'One sometimes sees one member speaking and another accompanying the speech with his actions. This I remarked more than once in a worthy old citizen, who was afraid of speaking himself, but when his neighbour spoke he accompanied every energetic sentence with a suitable gesticulation, by which means his whole body was sometimes in motion.'

Our visitor observes that the principal point in the debate is frequently lost in personal contests and bickerings; and that this sort of thing lasts till it has become tedious and tiresome. It would seem, from his description generally, that 'personal explanation' was more frequently necessary a century ago than it is now.

MORITZ had also the privilege of witnessing

the proceedings at a Westminster election. With a mind attuned to lofty views of things, derived from classic and poetical pursuits, he disdains to dwell upon the rowdyism and disorder while such lofty interests as the election of a popular representative are at stake. 'Whilst in Prussia,' he says, 'poets only speak of the love of country as one of the dearest of all human affections; here there is no man who does not feel and describe with rapture how much he loves his country. . . . All the enthusiasm of my earliest years, kindled by the patriotism of the illustrious heroes of Rome—Coriolanus, Julius Cæsar, Antony—were now revived in my mind, and though all I had just seen and heard be, in fact, but the semblance of liberty, yet at that moment I thought it charming, and it warmed my heart. Yes, depend upon it when you here see how in this happy country the lowest and meanest member of society thus unequivocally testifies the interest which he takes in everything of a public nature; when you see how even women and children bear a part in the great

Foreign Visitors in England.

concerns of their country; in short, how high and low, rich and poor, all concur in declaring their feelings and their convictions that a carter, a common tar, or a scavenger, is still a man—nay, an Englishman, and as such has his rights and privileges defined and known as exactly and as well as his King—take my word for it, you will feel yourself very differently affected from what you are when staring at our soldiers in their exercises at Berlin.'

There is something of singular simplicity, mingled with sound good sense, about MORITZ'S letters to his friend at home, and some courage must be attributed to one who could make use of the comparison involved in this last sentence while Frederick the Great yet lived and reigned.

Our parliamentary system would appear to be regarded as something peculiarly unique; something that cannot any way be copied by another people. This is observable from generation to generation. 'The greater number of nationalities have adapted the system to their own standard and requirements. Not one has copied in their entirety the exterior forms of their model; and there will appear nothing surprising in the fact when we consider that these forms are the effigies—sometimes grotesque and almost all superannuated—of historical or pre-historic traditions special to the Anglo-Saxon race.' A true enough observation from one of the latest commentators on our institutions, DARYL, tinged with just enough of that impatient flippancy which is characteristic of many modern minds in their inability to understand the value and the strength of time-honoured traditions. There is an obvious unwillingness to believe it possible for liberty really to exist in a system which has not yet had the privilege of being turned topsy-turvy. The author just quoted, studying 'public life in England' for ten years or so, has provided abundant proof of his acquaintance with our institutions; but his approval is lukewarm, and he frankly discusses the future as though it were big with changes, notwithstanding our 'hierarchic sentiment.' DARYL has sketched several prominent Liberals, but does not appear to have discovered a 'fine conscience,' or a decent orator, among the members of the opposite party. And it is quite new to be informed that in the Upper House there are 'scarcely thirty politicians worthy of the name.'

It should be granted that M. DARYL's chapter on the House of Commons is one of the very best sketches of the procedure, and of the outward and visible signs, of parliamentary life.

The foreigner who has followed political life in England with the most seriousness is, perhaps, VON RAUMER. In his book ('England in 1835') he returns freshly to every question that is agitating the country in Parliament. He has tried to understand what he is writing about, and has tolerably succeeded; and shows little of the disposition—so common among our critics, and so characteristic of superficial observers—to lay down abstract theories for our improvement. In this, perhaps, lies the secret of Von RAUMER's unalloyed enjoyment of his trip to England. He came with the determination to see all that was best to be seen, and to make the best of all that he did see. Here, for example, is a passage from one of his letters, at once philosophic and homely, written just after the death of William Cobbett; at the close of a period when that worthy had been, for some time past, the foremost of a series of earnest politicians who made themselves heard from the very depths of the crowd, yet who had not altogether succeeded in attaining that coherent utterance which is usually demanded by political theorists: 'These men,' he says, 'thought, lived, felt like plebeians, and therefore found an echo in the people; and it would have been more rational to investigate the causes of this than to make it a subject of lamentation. Instead of wasting their time in fruitless abuse, people would then discover means of redressing real evils, of showing the groundlessness of false complaints, and of exhibiting absurdities in all their nakedness. If there be any individuals who think to turn the democratical heritage of these men to account, they will probably find themselves mistaken. The spirit of resistance to power, which grows with rank luxuriance on the rough uncultured soil of the people, has a native life which, when trained and pruned, bears the noblest fruit, such, for instance, as heroic devotion to country. On the other hand, the revolutionary tendency which is nurtured in the closet, which borrows all its force from the annihilation of the positive, and thinks to lead nations captive with a few phrases, is shallow in its origin, presumptuous in its course, destructive in its results. Popular life is far too rich, varied, earnest, vivid, to be long chained to the dry bones of a superficial system. Their sorrows and their joys are not to be learned from the political herbariums of system-mongers; and when once it comes to blows, there are thoughts and feelings in motion that are not dreamt of in the philosophy of these political pedagogues.' This is really admirable; and this passage from VON RAUMER is one of the tokens which distinguish the mind of a man free from party-bias—a quality so little regarded by the majority of our intelligent visitors as to be almost absent.

CHAPTER VIII.

Our National Character.

THERE is one comprehensive topic, upon which all our intelligent visitors are found competent (at least, in their own eyes) to give decisive opinions. These opinions vary in quality, in candour, in temper, in manner; but they are, above all, decisive. Everyone has settled, without hesitation, his views upon our national character. It is, naturally, a topic the most interesting to us as a nation; but when we find that the varieties of disposition given to Englishmen extend to every shade, from that of near perfection down to one of almost absolute wickedness, the question becomes truly entertaining.

It is impossible for any intelligent person

making a study of these foreign visitors without attributing to them certain individualities. They all betray themselves. We feel that we have met their counterparts.

There, for example, is the snarling priest, 'wiser in his own eyes than ten men who can render a reason,' who has reached our shores ready-primed for complaint and depreciation at every turn. Because we have left the bosom of mother Church, *i.e.*, no longer believe the same as he does, we are capricious, gloomy, and fanatical; we are 'eaten up with avarice;' we are fierce and cruel, in the gall of bitterness and in the bond of iniquity. He stares with what he thinks is intelligent wonder, but is only stupidity. He has come with his prejudices, bent on making every feature reflect them, and every word and action justify them. Another, such as SORBIERE, having much good disposition about him, is possessed nevertheless with a sort of instinct that Providence has selected him to set the world quite straight. With a certain amount of good sense, he yet has his nose in the air, sniffing at a people who have not been educated in the same way as himself, and voting them detestable; thus turning an opportunity of wise self-instruction into one of useless carping at things strange.

On the other hand, such a one as the gentle MORITZ finds his delight in showing how much pleasure he derives from his journey. He has his proportion of failures and blunders, and does not exaggerate them to the discredit of Englishmen; he sometimes meets with ill behaviour, but is ready to believe that it is partly occasioned by his own inexperience. He looks at everything with even too much sentiment, and has rather the characteristic known as 'simple-minded.' Most Germans, to judge from the inevitable preface to their books, show that they have previously made themselves acquainted with former travels in this country before committing themselves to the journey. MORITZ does not actually say as much, but it is clear that he has not only read something about England, but has made himself acquainted with her literature. This is so different from the average Frenchman. With some exceptions, the Frenchman has visited our shores primed with 'hearsay,' and nothing deeper. It is true, there are instances in recent times of a French gentleman's account of England being actually occasioned by the demerits of another which he has discovered to be unjust. Monsieur GROSLEY's 'Londres,' the work of a learned and philosophic mind, was, perhaps, the first systematic and thorough account of English manners and customs and character which obtained the honours of general recognition. But another generation arose, which lamented the errors into which he had fallen, and was anxious to do more justice to the theme. In our own times, ESQUIROS gives us an exhaustive study of England and its people, the fruit of many years' study and residence among us. In no department of human inquiry is it so necessary for the observer to restrain his tendency to self-exaltation as in the estimate to be made of strangers, above all the strangers of another land. Yet, such is human perversity, nine travellers out of ten habitually think what they are predisposed to think; and it may be safely said that the shorter the period devoted to the inquiry, the more dogmatic and erroneous is the verdict.

A sound patriotic spirit is universally remarked in the English character. Our alleged harshness toward strangers is credited to a perverse direction which this spirit sometimes takes. But it is to be noticed that this charge is instigated, in general, by those persons only who have seen little of the country. For example, SULLY, whose embassy to James I. was not of long duration, and who made some friends here, and learned to admire much that he saw, could write in this astoundingly ill-tempered vein : ' It is certain that the English hate us, and this hatred is so general and inveterate that one would almost be tempted to number it among their natural dispositions. It is undoubtedly an effect of their arrogance and pride ; for no nation in Europe is more haughty and insolent, nor more conceited of its superior excellence. Were they to be believed, understanding and common-sense are to be found only among them. They are obstinately wedded to all their own opinions, and despise those of any other nation; and to hear others, or suspect themselves, is what never enters into their thoughts.' Now, as a marked contrast to this, let us compare this with what MURALT says (near a century later), who stayed here for a not much longer period, but who saw little of the Court and more of the middle classes. He notes the same facts as SULLY, and manages, nevertheless, to convey a quite different impression of this side of the English character. He says: 'I have not remarked any insolence among them to strangers—at least in the common affairs of life; so that I cannot see any reason for distinguishing them from other nations, on that score; and, generally speaking, their ways are far from being so harsh or disagreeable to us as most people imagine. They do not trouble themselves much about us, when they don't know us; and when they do, they make us sensible sometimes that they love themselves best. That is enough; they are strongly prepossessed in favour of their own nation. This influences all their discourse and ways, and affords matter of complaint to strangers; and perhaps the folly of the greatest part of the world may be imputed to the same error.'

The Abbé LE BLANC discourses very considerately on our supposed excess of prejudice in favour of our own land. He plainly asserts that it exists, both in the language of poets and authors and in that of the common people; only that the former 'are more modest in their expressions.'

'The love of our country,' he says, 'which nature has engrafted on every heart, is one of the most useful virtues to the support of the community; but it is with this as with many others—our vanity may blend some vicious tincture with it that may alter its purity. Nothing is proof against this taint of self-love. Prejudices sometimes render this attachment to one's native soil ridiculous in particular instances, which is so commendable in general. It is more difficult than is imagined to get rid of these national prejudices, which injure our reason, and hinder us from putting ourselves

Foreign Visitors in England. 129

in a true point of light to form a right judgment of objects not familiar to us. . . . The power of habit hurries us away, and makes us condemn manners which have no other defect but that of not being our own. Accustomed to the hat, the turban shocks us; simplicity passes for rudeness with those who do not reflect how much of the arbitrary enters into what is called politeness; we laugh at that of the Chinese, without considering that they have the same right to laugh at ours. And, indeed, when a person loves his country—and, what is still more ridiculous, without loving it—he is unjust with regard to others.' And he further implies that his own fellow-countrymen may possibly deserve as much reproach as the English in respect of their national prejudices; and, admitting that the English have the fault of supposing that they alone are in possession of all the virtues, he is sorry to have to confess that it cannot be said of the Frenchmen as it can of the English, that they generally speak as modestly of themselves as they do proudly of their country. 'A Frenchman seems to esteem his nation only with respect to himself; an Englishman appears not to set any value on himself, but with respect to his nation; which gives an air of vanity to the one, and to the other an air of greatness.'

After long reflection on this subject, no one will come to any other decision than this: that the whole idea of our 'national vanity' is exaggerated. Most persons who came to English shores, before our naval and mercantile supremacy made it obvious to the world what stuff we were made off, came with the fixed notion that the English people had but moderate abilities for anything but fighting. We were not highly civilized; and we had the very great demerit of living in a somewhat inaccessible country. The Straits of Dover have much to account for in the old imperfect estimates of our character. It is a universal tendency of human nature to decry and to depreciate that which we know nothing of; and many writers previous to the seventeenth century are betrayed into this tendency.

So, when these intelligent, but sometimes

vain-glorious, strangers land here, and find a race of intrepid and self-reliant people not less polished and often better-informed than themselves, who have a history of centuries, during which more personal liberty has existed than in any other country of Europe, and whose whole political and social daily existence breathes an independent spirit, it is too much for them to bear. Rather than acknowledge the superiority which, in some respects, is at once obvious, and which bursts upon them a little unexpectedly, the visitor resorts to his bundle of prejudices, applies this or that to the objects and persons encountered, and thus produces a defective and distorted picture. Perhaps this is a fault which belongs still to the average traveller, but it is more obvious in the French than in any other. Americans are, too, somewhat given to a petulant way, born of the discovery that there are still some things done in the old country remarkably well, and that there are still some Englishmen who prefer their own institutions to American ones. The absorbing interest of many objects in this country, and the real affection and reverence which Americans have expressed for its historic features, do not always hinder them from displaying a spirit almost amounting to arrogance. They can pardon no vain-glory but their own. One of the most comical things in the whole of this literature of English travel is a sentence of HAWTHORNE's (at Chester): 'An American must always have imagined a better cathedral than this!' HAWTHORNE, in common with others from the United States, repeatedly gives vent to his belief that Englishmen hate Americans, although there may be some individual cases of mutual regard. But it is difficult to imagine how he could justify the following remark (unless Liverpool folk are widely different from Londoners): 'It is very queer, the resolute quizzing of our manners, when we are really and truly much better figures, and with much better capacity of polish for drawing-room or dining-room than they are. I had been struck on my arrival at Smithell's Hall by the very rough aspect of these John Bulls in their morning garb, their coarse frock-coats, gray hats, checked trousers, and stout shoes. At dinner-table it was not at first easy to recognise the same individuals in their white waistcoats, muslin cravats, thin black coats, with silk facings perhaps. But after a while you see the same rough figure through all the finery, and become sensible that John Bull cannot make himself fine, whatever he may put on. He is a rough animal, and his female is well adapted to him.'

One may seek in vain for a very long time something to account for this rather unkind turn. It is grotesque as well as unkind. The American visitor or dweller in London is usually credited with a little extra self-conceit, unaccompanied by prejudice; and that is entirely justified by the circumstance that the average American found in London is a successful, and pretty often a wealthy, man. But it is a jaundiced view of the case to represent us as habitually seeking to lower his social qualities by false conceptions. There will be always a sense of rivalry between the two nations; but it is absurd and unjust

134 *Foreign Visitors in England.*

on either hand to suspect that the other is on the watch for deficiences of manner and personal peccadilloes. And this passage, quoted from HAWTHORNE, serves but to show how the best of men look when they allow the genial side of their nature to disappear under the influence of some temporary ill-humour. Professor HOPPIN, another visitor of our own days, in the midst of some picturesque description, suddenly plunges into a study of English character, in the course of which he lets a little light into this mutual suspicion. He says, 'I have found in travelling in England that if I could chastise my own intemperate nationality, and not let it stick out offensively, that I soon made friends with Englishmen who, in the end, would volunteer more in reference to their own failings than I should ever have thought of producing to them. Mutual pride prevents Englishmen and Americans from seeing each other's good traits and positive resemblances. And all Englishmen are not disagreeable, neither are all Americans insufferable. There are the pleasantest and sweetest people in the world in both nations; so there are undoubtedly the most insolent and contemptible.'

We must credit MISSON with one of the most gracious expressions regarding the outward demeanour of Englishmen. 'Other nations' (he says) 'accuse the common people among the English of incivility, because they generally accost one another without putting their hands to their hats, and without that flood of compliments that usually pours out of the mouth of the French, the Italians, etc. But they take the thing in a wrong light; the idea of the English is that civility does not consist wholly of these outward shows, which very often are hypocritical and deceitful. . . . I am willing to believe that the English are subject to certain faults, as no doubt all nations are; but, everything considered, I am satisfied by several years' experience that the more strangers are acquainted with the English, the more they will esteem and love them. What brave men do I know in England! What moderation! What generosity! What uprightness of heart! What piety and charity! Yes, there are in England persons that may truly be called accomplished: men who are wisdom and goodness itself.' After this one need not despair. This, from the pen of one whom it must have cost something to 'unlearn contempt,' as Whittier would say, makes one hope that the difficulty of understanding us is not insurmountable. Happily there is some further testimony to the effect that when the chilly, phlegmatic, melancholy exterior of the average Englishman is once removed, an unequalled warmth, and fervency, and cheerfulness is discovered.

Before dismissing this topic we may select a few of the summaries of the English character. Some of them are oddly contradictory in themselves, and some are suspiciously at second-hand. Some are obviously tempered with prejudice, and others are as unmistakably the effusions of generous and kindly natures, who found in this country far more of sympathetic welcome and courteous treatment than by hearsay they had been led to expect.

'The English are so cunning and faithless that a foreigner would not be sure of his life among them. A Briton is not to be trusted on his bended knees.'—(Sasek, journalist of VON ROZMITAL.)

'Every gentleman and every worthy person showed unto me all points of most friendly courtesy, and, taking me first by the hand, lovingly embraced and bad me right heartily welcome.'—(LEMNIUS.)

'The people are bold, courageous, ardent and cruel in war, fiery in attack, and having little fear of death; they are not vindictive, but very inconstant, rash, vain-glorious, light and deceiving, and very suspicious, especially of foreigners, whom they despise. They are full of courtly and affected manner of words, which they take for gentility, civility, and wisdom. They are eloquent, and very hospitable; they feed well and delicately, and eat a great deal of meat, and, as the Germans pass the bounds of sobriety in drinking, these do the same in eating.'—(VAN METEREN.)

'The common people of London, giving way to their natural inclination, are proud, arrogant, and uncivil to foreigners; against whom, and especially the French, they entertain a great prejudice, treating such as come among them with contempt and insult.

'The nobility, though also proud, have not so usually the defects of the lower orders, displaying a certain degree of politeness and courtesy towards strangers; and this is still more the case with those gentlemen who have been out of the kingdom and travelled, they having taken a lesson in politeness from the manners of other nations. Almost all of them speak French and Italian, and readily apply themselves to learn the latter language from the goodwill which they entertain toward our nation; and although by their civil treatment of foreign gentlemen, whom they endeavour to imitate, they moderate a little that stiffness or uncouthness which is peculiar to them; yet they fail in acquiring such good manners as to put them on a level with the easy gentility of the Italians, not being able to get the better of a certain natural melancholy, which has the appearance of eternally clouding their minds with unpleasant thoughts.

'The English in general are by nature proud and phlegmatic, and patient in their behaviour, so that they never hurry those who work for them by an indiscreet impatience, but suffer them to go on at their own pleasure and according to their ability. This proceeds from their melancholy temperament, for which those who live in the North of England are more remarkable than those in the South; the former being saturnine, and the latter somewhat more lively. They consider a long time before they come to a determination; but having once decided their resolution is irrevocable, and they maintain their opinion with the greatest obstinacy.

'The English are men of a handsome countenance and shape, and of an agreeable complexion, which is attributable to the temperature of the climate, to the nature of their food, and to the use of beer rather than wine, and, above all to the salubrity of the air, which is almost always clear; that thick atmosphere, which is seen from a distance hovering over London, not being caused by corrupt vapours, but arising casually from the smoke of the mineral coal from Scotland, which issues from the chimneys, etc.

'Of a most manly spirit, and valiant in war both by land and sea, to a degree that amounts almost to rashness.'—(Count MAGALOTTI.)

'The English may be easily brought to anything, provided you fill their bellies, let them have freedom of speech, and do not bear too hard upon their lazy temper.'—(SORBIERE.)

The inhabitants of this excellent country are tall, handsome, well made, fair, active, robust, courageous, thoughtful, devout, lovers of the liberal arts, and as capable of the sciences as any people in the world.'—(MISSON.)

'The commonalty are rude and cruel, addicted to thieving and robbing, faithless, headstrong, inclined to strife and mutiny, gluttonous, and superstitiously addicted to the predictions of foolish astrologers; in short, of a very extravagant temper, delighting in the noise of guns, drums, and bells, as if it were some sweet harmony.'—(Dr. GEMELLI-CARERI.)

'In England the belly always takes the place of the back.'—(MURALT.)

So much for short generalizations. After the period of this writer our visitors get more prosy. They are immersed in detail, and they descend into the very depths of things. The Abbé LE BLANC's bulky work is a veritable encyclopædia of the ways, manners, industries, frivolities, and prejudices of the English, compared with those of the French. Much the same may be said of M. GROSLEY's endeavour to present a full picture of society in London. GROSLEY's 'Londres' remained a text-book for the study of English life and character until the end of the eighteenth century.

CHAPTER IX.

Our National Character—*continued*.

IT must be admitted to be with justice that the English nation is credited with a tendency to fanaticism. We hear much, throughout the ages, of the melancholy of the English; one of its causes is our fanatical rage, which leads us to extremes before we have reflected upon the consequences. The English know no medium in anything,' says one.

In support of this opinion, reference is usually made by our visitors to the consequences of Wycliffe's intrepidity, to the party conflicts under the Tudors, andto the wholesale demoralization of public opinion under the Stuarts. The roots and branches of sectarianism are a favourite topic. Monsieur

GROSLEY enters largely into it; although he does not appear to think that it matters so much, to the sectarian himself, what is the quality and character of his belief, as is the need for producing his belief unto the bitter end. 'Hell is,' he remarks, 'the favourite topic of the Methodist preachers, who, we are told, contribute thereby to people Bedlam.' He observes that the English carry all their passions to excess; and the stubborn temper of the people, having its imagination kindled by superstition, naturally proceeds to extremity. Hence the great number and variety and extravagance of the sects. The papist GEMELLI-CARERI is horror-struck with this phase of what he considers irreligion. The accomplished narrator of COSMO's journey is moderate and dignified, but none the less severe and contemptuous, over the religious divisions of England; and he devotes many pages to a description of them, according to the accounts which he has received in response to his inquiries.

The Abbé LE BLANC is rather amused than not by the heat and rancour engendered by sectarianism. 'The sermons of the different parties,' he says, 'are commonly a sort of hostilities which they commit against each other; and treat more of controversy than of morality.' The consequence of these disputes thus tends to inspire men's hearts with sentiments quite the reverse of Christian. He retails an anecdote, indecorous enough, showing the estimate in which he held sectarian disputes: 'Two honest Englishmen, one a devout and constant hearer of a preacher of the Established Church, and the other a zealous attendant at the meetings of a Presbyterian teacher, appointed to meet at a tavern to discourse on some points of doctrine which those two ministers had preached on the Sunday before. . . . A bottle of French wine was brought, and one of them proposed *Predestination*. After several bumpers the dispute grew warm; and the texts of Scripture, and quotations from the Fathers, made such a noise that two low women—who are but too frequently found in the taverns of London—brought thither by the uproar, resolved to enter the room and put an end to it at once.

Foreign Visitors in England.

At the sight of these miserable wretches the heat of the dispute immediately subsided; our doctors changed the conversation, and libertinism succeeded to controversy. But the girls were soon sent away, and our worthy disputants resumed the bottle and predestination. The quarrel became greater than ever, and their animosity increased in proportion as the fumes of the wine flew into their heads. At last they were quite drunk, and disputed till they drew their swords to end the controversy; and if the disturbance had not happily brought somebody into the room, in all probability predestination had brought them both to a tragical end.'

Political partisanship, another species of fanaticism observed by our visitors of the seventeenth and eighteenth centuries, affords much amusement. Similar stories to the above are told of the useless personal conflicts engendered by party strife.

To the reaction consequent upon fanaticism is partly attributed our national habits of melancholy. Some writers dwell long and learnedly upon our gloomy and melancholy ways when not excited either by passion or by healthy, violent exercise. GROSLEY finds in English religious exercises a direct incentive to gloom, although he is willing to attribute some of it to the fogs, with which he finds the country is perpetually overcast. There appears to be a prevailing belief that there is something in the physical constitution of Englishmen which renders them a prey to fits of melancholia; and the drinking of beer is alleged to be contributory thereto. The somewhat violent bodily exercises to which Englishmen submit are supposed to have become necessary in order to escape these tendencies. Another favourite idea, allied to this last, entertained by nearly every Frenchman who visits our shores, is that we are prone to suicide. It would be a curious inquiry to trace and compare their various theories on this subject. They always assume that suicide is more frequent in England than elsewhere, although it is extremely likely that statistics would not support the notion.

GROSLEY actually 'congratulates the French upon its being unknown to their forefathers,' and suggests that this crime should continue to be the undisturbed inheritance of the Italians and the English. He goes so far as to maintain that care is taken to block up the avenues to the river-side, in order to remove that temptation which would inevitably assault a Londoner at sight of the water. Yet 'what precautions,' he asks, 'can prevent those who are resolved to die from carrying their purpose into execution? That it is impossible to prevent this mischief I am convinced by the shocking sight of twenty skulls which were found in the bed of the Thames, where they were digging the foundation for the first piles of the new bridge!' It is difficult to believe at first that this is serious; but from the grave way in which he continues to discuss the subject, it is clear that this is one of the prejudices he brought with him which he is unable to shake off.

LE BLANC remarks that cheerfulness is much wanting in English society. 'Nothing is so uncommon among the English as that sweetness of temper and cheerfulness of humour, which are the charms of society, and they are great losers for want of them. They would be much happier if they were more social.' He says, again: 'When I see an Englishman laugh, I fancy I see him hunting after joy rather than having caught it. . . . A laugh leaves no more traces on their countenance than a flash of lightning on the face of the heavens.' He has discovered a set of men in England who 'never laugh at all, and those are the Presbyterians; they make laughing to be the eighth mortal sin. . . . There are families of them who have never laughed for two or three generations.' The climate of the country is credited with some share of this. There seems to be an almost unanimous feeling, indeed, on the part of our gayer neighbours, that fogs and Puritanism have together overcast the nation, and made it less happy than it deserves to be.

Some of our friends find the English people excessively variable, cheerful by turns, and nothing long. A rather pettish passage from SULLY, who otherwise had many good reasons for satisfaction with the demeanour of the English toward him, will illustrate this view. There is doubtless some truth in what he says. But it is ill-humoured, and does not altogether agree with what he has said elsewhere: 'Sometimes one would be induced to think they have contracted all the instability of the element by which they are surrounded; with them all things must submit to the reigning disposition; and the sole difference between them and the most inconstant people of Europe is, that their inconstancy proceeds not from lightness, but from their vanity, which continually shows itself in a thousand different shapes. Their self-love renders them slaves to all their capricious humours. What they at one time believe to have wisely performed, or firmly resolved, is at another time destroyed without their knowing it, or being able to give a reason for it. They are accordingly so undetermined in themselves that frequently one would not take them for the same persons, and hence they themselves sometimes appear surprised on perceiving their own continued irresolution.' Monsieur MURALT alludes more pleasantly to the changeable humours of the English, and expresses his opinion that they 'would not appear more unsteady than other people were it not that they take less pains to bridle their thoughts, and dare to let the world see what they really are.' POLLNITZ is still more generous toward our weaknesses of character. He finds little fault with the average Englishman, except for some unevenness of temper; and if you don't take notice of that 'he will soon come to himself.

CHAPTER X.

Sunday in England.

THE puritanical observance of Sunday is regarded as a singular defect in our social organization. It is even held by some writers to have a perceptible operation in moulding the English character. It would be difficult to find a single visitor from the Continent who attempts to excuse it, or one who is able to understand the principle at all. There is an ironic tone about references to it, as though Englishmen could not possibly be quite right in their minds, who consecrate the major part of their only day of rest and recreation to mere gloomy inaction, even under the specious pretence of devoting it to holy meditation. MISSON, of course, makes merry over it: 'I believe their doctrine upon this head does not differ from ours, but most assuredly our scruples are much less than theirs. This appears on a hundred occasions. I have observed it particularly in the printed confessions of persons that are hanged; Sabbath-breaking is the crime the poor wretches always begin with. If they had killed father and mother, they would not mention that article till after having professed how often they had broke the Sabbath. One of the good old English customs on the Sabbath-day is to feast as nobly as possible, and especially not to forget the pudding. It is a common practice, even among people of good substance, to have a huge piece of roast beef on Sundays, of which they stuff till they can swallow no more, and eat the rest cold the other days of the week.' Without being as frivolous as this flighty Huguenot, our visitors one and all regard the English Sunday with amused wonder. Contempt for the system, and pity for the poor Londoner especially, finds renewed expression up to our own times. Perhaps the best (because so very temperate) outpouring on

Foreign Visitors in England.

the subject is that of von Raumer (1835). He says: 'People of education doubtless fill this day in a varied and intellectual manner. The lower classes, who often have to toil wearily through every other day, find Sunday the weariest of all. Often, after serving an austere master, they are made to see in the Father of Love an austerer still. Singing, music, dancing, the drama, and all amusements which are addressed to our intellectual nature, are forbidden, and denounced as schools of the devil. What is the consequence? That people of temperate, regular habits conduct themselves in a temperate and regular manner; while a great number of the less sedate and less patient of restraint give themselves up to the grossest sensual enjoyment, and seek in that the distinction between Sunday and working-day. One set of people complain of the desecration of the Sabbath—and in this they are perfectly right; but the only means they can devise for the remedy of the evil are still severer laws; and in this, in my opinion, they are quite wrong. If all public-houses and gin-shops could be entirely closed on a Sunday, what would the common people do then? How would they get rid of their intolerable ennui? By spiritual exercises? But are not two sermons, two services of religion, sufficient? Are they not as much as the mind of an ordinary man can bear? By reading? Many cannot read, and more have no books which they care to read. By sleeping? Or what? In this way we should arrive at the conclusion that, to avoid all these disorders, some millions of people ought every Sunday to be chained or locked up.'

Monsieur GROSLEY observes that in England the influence of religion on grown persons is a 'new source of melancholy'; that the Jewish rigour with which they are obliged to keep the Sabbath, the only holiday they have, is an absolute specific to nourish their gloomy temper; that 'the religious exercises of the English afford to children nothing capable of softening and humanizing their disposition.' This is of similar tenor to the remarks of foreigners generally during the seventeenth and eighteenth centuries, to the effect that we had become a less religious people since the Reformation. The long prayers which seemed never to end, and the metaphysical and dogmatical sermons, offered nothing to strike the senses or arouse feeling. Religious ardour was absorbed in party conflicts. The numerous sects were occupied in denouncing one another. The clergy of all denominations were, with some exceptions, of a low order: 'their sermons more respected than their persons.' Those of the Establishment naturally drew more notice to their outward conduct. Yet VOLTAIRE says that the English clergy had more 'regular' morals than the priests in France : while he found the more respectable part of the order lived 'very much on the reserve, most of them being pedants.' There is, doubtless, some exaggeration in several statements as to their frequenting the London coffee-houses, 'often with a pipe in their mouth.' The coffee-houses were places of resort, especially for personal appointments. Within the memory of the present generation, there still remained one, the Chapter Coffee-house, in

Paternoster Row, which held its character as a house-of-call for country parsons and others long after it had actually ceased to be so.

As for tobacco-smoking in itself, and considered with reference to those persons who have a right to indulge in the 'care-dispelling weed,' it is unfair to withhold it from the parson, of all people. If a sermon is anything at all, it has exhausted certain energies; and the best introduction to a restorative is, doubtless, a sedative. Besides, MISSON has pointed out that tobacco makes profound theologians and very moral philosophers. None but a fanatic would dispute the point.

GROSLEY took the pains to try and understand how Sabbatarianism came to take such deep root in England, and hints a sincere regret that James I. and his successor could not prevail in the endeavour to lessen the rigour of the bonds which Puritanism had wrung from the two immediately preceding sovereigns. He finds that Protestants could as easily make use of pious frauds as could the Papists, when there was a purpose to serve; and that pious frauds are not unknown among the contemners of Sabbath-breaking. Monsieur GROSLEY is sedate and philosophic throughout his book. But he is very near being tempted to be merry when he comes to this topic. He notices that the tolls are doubled, that the watermen cease to ply and newspapers are discontinued, when Sunday comes round; that no one dares to sing, or to play, or to dance; 'except in church time, the inhabitants of London wait, with their arms across, till service is again celebrated, or till the day is over, without having any other amusement but to gaze in a melancholy mood at those who pass to and fro in the streets.' This is on a par with the very neat observation of the author of the 'Voyage Philosophique' (which would be spoilt in translation): 'On est peu matinal dans ce pays, surtout des jours de fêtes qui sont consacrés à l'inaction sabbatique, très-religieusement observée.'

But it is among more recent travellers that Sabbatarianism is treated with most freedom. There are even some who approach a tone of mockery, at finding a whole nation condemned to lose its weekly day of recreation at the bidding of a minority. Dr. CARUS hints that we begin with the 'fourth commandment' because we find it easier to observe than many others. Let us hope there is less truth than wit in this very suggestive remark.

With the exception of a few gentlemen of the cloth from America, the whole system is treated with more or less of contempt by our visitors. TAINE's first day in London was a Sunday: probably the unhappiest day he ever spent in his life. He has evidently heard, beforehand, of English Sundays, and he must needs confirm the doleful tale. He is ready for suicide after an hour's walk past the closed shops. Everything is gloomy and sooty. Somerset House is a frightful thing. Nelson is hideous, like a rat impaled upon the top of a pole,—and so forth. He quotes a fellow-countryman's words to the effect that 'Here religion spoils one day out of seven, and destroys the seventh part of possible happiness,' and doesn't appear to disapprove the idea. It is pretty certain, at any rate, that Monsieur TAINE recovered his spirits on the following day, when he found the world moving on again.

CHAPTER XI.

Eating and Drinking.—Cookery.—Toasts.—Beer.—Tobacco.

HE difficulty of pleasing 'everybody' is not oftener exemplified than in connection with affairs of the stomach. And, as a topic upon which prejudices are easily aroused, it is not surprising that our intelligent visitors have much to say upon the food and drink of Englishmen, in some cases with flat disapproval; but more generally with the air of persons who have found, in the substantial and profuse character of the English dinner-table, some solace for the absence of taste in its preparation. Nor is there an entire want of approval on this latter score. POLLNITZ, for example, declares that at private houses in London 'the tables are served with as much

taste and delicacy as in any country in the world.' This gentleman praises the roast beef of England, and proclaims his 'love for their puddings.' But he is not supported by the declared tastes of other travellers. The big joints of beef or mutton are regarded as distinctive accompaniments of the grossness of our national tastes. MURALT regards it an emblem of the prosperity and plenty of the country to see a great piece of thirty or forty pounds' weight of roast beef, 'the favourite dish as well at the King's table as at a tradesman's.' Monsieur GROSLEY must have been unfortunate in his experience of family cookery; for having eaten meat in all the different shapes in which it is served up to table, that is to say, roast and boiled, 'I could find in it neither the consistence, the juice, nor the exquisiteness of that of France. Their fowls are soft and flabby; the veal has all the imperfection of flesh not completely formed; the mutton has nothing to recommend it but its fat,' etc. MISSON calls the English mutton 'not so good as ours in France; it has quite another taste.' SORBIERE makes a few quaint remarks, which seem to indicate some chronic failure of digestion. He says: 'The English are not very dainty, and the greatest lords' tables who do not keep French cooks are covered only with large dishes of meat: they are strangers to bisks and pottage; only once I saw some milk-pottage in a large and deep dish, some of which, as a singular favour, the master of the house gave in a china dish to some of his guests. Their pastry is coarse and ill-baked; their stewed fruits and confectionery-ware cannot be eaten.' As pastry-making is, and always was, a fine art, SORBIERE may have been right enough in noticing the work of bungling fingers; but it is probable that he had slender opportunities, perhaps none at all, of seeing the pastries of the country-side. He is not supported generally in his views on our pastry. English puddings, again, are regarded as a great national speciality. 'I am in love with their puddings' (says POLLNITZ), 'which are made of flour, eggs, crumbs of bread, and, in short, a thousand ingredients that I know nothing of; but all together makes very good fare.' MISSON describes the composition of a Christmas pie as a great nostrum in every family; 'it is a most learned mixture of neat's tongues, chicken, eggs, sugar, raisins, lemon and orange peel, various kinds of spicery, etc. They also make a sort of soup with plums, not at all inferior to the pie, which is in their language called plum-porridge.' MISSON's gastronomic turn leads him to make many casual allusions to our food and cookery. Under the heading '*Table*' he has summarised his ideas in a truly comical, and, perhaps, tolerably accurate vein. He thus discourses on this universal topic:

'The English eat a great deal at dinner; they rest awhile, and to it again, till they have quite stuffed their paunch. Their supper is moderate: gluttons at noon, and abstinent at night. I always heard they were great flesh-eaters, and I found it true. I have known several people in England that never eat any bread, and universally they eat very little; they nibble a few crumbs, while they chew the meat by whole mouthfuls. Generally speaking, the English tables are not delicately served. There are some noblemen that have both French and English cooks, and these eat much after the French manner. But among the middling sort of people (which are those I spoke of before), they have ten or twelve sorts of common meats, which infallibly take their turns at their tables, and two dishes are their dinners: a pudding, and a piece of roast beef. Another time they will have a piece of boiled beef, and then they salt it some days beforehand, and besiege it with five or six heaps of cabbage, carrots, turnips, or some other herbs or roots, well peppered and salted, and swimming in butter. Two of these dishes, always served up one after the other, make the usual dinner of a substantial gentleman, or wealthy citizen. When they have boiled meat, there is sometimes one of the company that will have broth; this is a kind of soup, with a little oatmeal in it, and some leaves of thyme or sage, or other such small herbs. They bring up this in as many porringers as there are people that desire it; those that please crumble a little bread into it, and this makes a kind of pottage.

'The pudding is a dish very difficult to be described, because of the several sorts there are of it; flour, with eggs, butter, sugar, suet, marrow, raisins, etc., are the most common ingredients of a pudding. They bake them in an oven, they boil them with meat, they make them fifty several ways. Blessed be he that invented pudding! for it is a manna that hits the palates of all sorts of people; a manna better than that of the wilderness, because the people are never weary of it. Ah, what an excellent thing is an English pudding! *To come in pudding time*, is as much as to say, to come in the most lucky moment in the world. Give an Englishman a pudding, and he shall think it a noble treat in any part of the world. . . . It would be unjust to take, in a rigorous sense, all that I have said of these common dishes; for the English eat everything that is produced naturally, as well as any other nation. I say *naturally*, in opposition to the infinite multitude of our made dishes; for they dress their meat much plainer than we do.'

Monsieur GROSLEY launches forth into encomiums on the quality of English bread, and notices that a very great deal of bread is consumed here. He observes that Londoners live principally upon tea and bread-and-butter until three or four o'clock in the afternoon. 'The slices are so thin' (he adds) 'that it does as much honour to the address of the person that cuts it, as to the sharpness of the knife.' Madame BOCAGE observes somewhere that 'Their drink is beer, and their food bread-and-butter.' PERLIN (a hundred and fifty years earlier) notes that the English eat much whiter bread than that commonly made in France. GROSLEY continues his theme on bread, with an account of the efforts formerly tried in Paris to make it with yeast, in the English fashion.

The Abbé LE BLANC informs us that the way of living in London fell heavily upon him more than once, notwithstanding the restraint he constantly exercised. The habit of sitting after dinner, drinking and toasting, he thought a useless and melancholy affair. The temptation to excess disgusted him. He sees that a good butler is thought more of than the confectioner, and seems to regret that dessert is so shortened, and even neglected, as to deprive us of the best opportunity for elegant conversation. 'Even at tables where they serve desserts,' he says, 'they do but show them, and presently take away everything, even to the table-cloth. By this the English, whom politeness does not permit to tell the ladies their company is troublesome, give them notice to retire. . . . The table is immediately covered with mugs, bottles, and glasses; and often with pipes of tobacco. All things thus disposed, the ceremony of toasts begins; . . . perhaps the English derive this custom from the Goths, who are said to have been hard drinkers; and, if so, they have the glory of having brought it to greater perfection. The young man toasts his mistress's health; the honest tradesman, his correspondent's; and the grave ecclesiastic, his bishop's. As for the bishop, he has that of his primate; and the primate may, if he pleases, drink to his guests " Prosperity to the Protestant Cause," or any other toast he thinks proper. The master of the house is the person who begins these rounds, and is obliged to take care of their order and exactness; both with regard to the manner of giving and of drinking the toasts, and to prevent any deviation from the rule which obliges all the company to drink equally alike.

''Tis customary to toast the reigning beauties, even those they know only by sight; and by this means the coxcomb gives himself the air of a man of fortune. The ladies themselves are pleased at this, when they come to hear of it, as this public homage paid to their charms is a proof of their fame. . . . To make an encomium on a young beauty, they say "she is one of the first toasts in England." She, on the contrary, whose lilies and roses time has faded, is called a cast-off toast. A man would appear ridiculous to some sort of people, who should have the misfortune to give for his toast a beauty whose charms are faded. A man must be acquainted with the map of London not to commit such an absurdity.

'The men of learning in this country, though they submit themselves very little to the other customs of the nation, are very exact observers of this ceremony of toasts. They practise it frequently, and with the greatest solemnity. . . . I have had Bernoulli, Euler, Maupertuis, Buffon, toasted to me. If they dine in taverns, which are very much frequented at London by persons of all ranks, the toasts vary still more; very frequently, after having drunk to the health of their friends, they drink to the ruin and damnation of their enemies. There is then no sort of mad pranks they do not think of, to excite one another to drink.'

From the references made to these customs by our travellers, it is clear that they were regarded as peculiarly English. MISSON, indeed, remarks that in France the custom of drinking healths is out of date among people of any distinction, it being equally impertinent and ridiculous. Madame BOCAGE speaks of it without ill-nature: 'immediately after the pudding is despatched, they drink warm punch. After the dessert, especially in the country, the cloth is taken away, and the women retire. The table is of fine Indian wood, and very smooth; little round vessels, called sliders, which are of the same wood, serve to hold the bottles, and the guests can put them round as they think proper. The name of each different sort of wine is graved upon a plate of silver, fastened to the neck of the flask; the guests choose the liquor to which they give the preference, and drink it with as serious an air as if they were doing penance, at the same time drinking the healths of eminent persons and fashionable beauties; this they call toasting.' GROSLEY and others allege the origin of drinking the health to be entirely barbarous. He has learned that the Scotch Highlanders (who are still but half-civilised, and who live in eternal discord and faction), have preserved the custom in its original purity: 'Drinking to a person's health means that you request him to guard you while you are drinking. In consequence of this tacit entreaty, the person whom you drink to replies, "I will pledge you," or, "I will answer for it"; draws his dagger, fixes it on the table, and continues upon the watch till you have drunk off your glass and laid it down.' GROSLEY, as a man with habits of literary and historic research, is enabled to trace a parallel ceremony among his own French ancestors. PERLIN refers also to this drinking business very quaintly; and endeavours to reproduce, phonetically, the sounds uttered in the language, with which he was evidently quite unacquainted: 'In drinking or eating they will say to you above a hundred times, *drind iou*, which is, "I am going to drink to you"; and you should answer them in your language *iplaigiu*, which means, "I pledge you." If you would thank them in their language, you must say, *god tanque artelay*, which is to say, "I thank you with all my heart." When they are drunk, they will swear blood and death that you should drink all that is in your cup, and will say thus to you, *bigod sol drind iou agoud oin*.'

Monsieur JOREVIN is exceedingly disgusted to find, sometimes, that the custom of the country 'does not permit you to drink more than half the cup, which is filled up, and presented to him or her whose health you have drunk.' As this gentleman was a genuine traveller, and saw very much of the provinces, he met with a great deal of tavern life; and this observation is doubtless founded upon his experience as a tourist. He notices, by the way, that no kind of business is transacted in England without the intervention of pots of beer.

This topic deserves yet another reference, as one having the unfortunate distinction of being a specially characteristic feature of English national habits. We have in MISSON a serio-comic description, which surely must have been drawn from the life, of this important ceremony: 'To drink at table without drinking to somebody's health, especially among middling people, would be like drinking in a corner, and be reckoned a very rude action. There are two principal grimaces which are universally observed, upon this occasion, among persons of all degrees and conditions. The first is that the person whose health is drunk, if an inferior, or even an equal, must remain as still as a statue while the drinker is drinking. If, for instance, you are about to help yourself to something out of the dish, you must stop suddenly, lay aside your fork or spoon, and wait, without stirring any more than a stone, till the other has drunk. After which, the second grimace is to make him a low bow, to the great hazard of dipping your peruke into the sauce upon your plate. I own that to a stranger these customs seem ridiculous; he thinks nothing can be more pleasant than to see a man that is just going to chew a mouthful of victuals, cut a piece of bread, wipe his fingers, or anything of that nature, in a moment put on a grave, serious face, keep his eyes fixed upon the person that drinks his health, and grow as motionless as if he were taken with a universal palsy, or struck with a thunderbolt. As civility absolutely requires this respectful immobility in the patient, so there is some caution to be used on the part of the agent. When you would drink a man's health, you should first keep your eyes upon him for a moment, and give him time, if possible, to swallow his mouthful, that you may not reduce him to the perplexing and uneasy necessity of putting a sudden stop to his grinders, and so sitting a good while with his mouth crammed with a huge load of victuals; which, commonly getting all to one side, raises his cheek as high as an egg, so forming a large kind of a wen, often shining with grease, equally distorted and unseemly.'

It is maintained by some of our friends that clubs arose from the necessity of finding a regular place for drinking. This is a little too much, although Addison has said something to a similar effect. Yet Monsieur LE BLANC is perhaps near the truth, when he states that Englishmen did not cultivate sufficiently the society of women for the sake of elegant conversation, on account of our ancient habits of intemperance, and that the same inclination to intemperance in drinking gave birth to those societies or clubs which met in public-houses. 'In vain' (he adds), 'have some affected to grace these sorts of associations with the respectable name of academies; the time and place of meeting sufficiently let us into the knowledge of their business. All these societies, in a word, under the imposing names of Independents, Literati, Virtuosi, etc., are nothing more than clubs of topers.'

There is a universal chorus of appreciation on the subject of beer. From the earliest traveller to our shores, to the latest, a new sensation is recorded when he has tasted beer or ale, 'most pleasaunte in tast, and holesomly relised,' as a sixteenth-century translator has it. This is one of the few matters concerning which the visitor ignores everything but his own physical sensation. He writes as though he had reached a goal of satisfaction. 'Botterdel' is the choicest production of any known country. Cyder is also esteemed. JOREVIN, while in Worcestershire, was taken by surprise with a draught of cyder instead of beer, and 'did not know what to think of it.' Having asked his landlord where it was made, 'he answered me that it grew upon trees.' PERLIN mentions that with beer it was the custom to eat 'very soft saffron cakes, in which there are likewise raisins, which give a relish to the beer.' Count MAGALOTTI speaks of 'another sort of beer made with the body of a capon which is left to grow putrid along with the malt.' It must not be omitted, however, to note that our friends were acquainted with the subtle effects of a drop too much. There does not appear to be any record of a confession on the part of any, that he was himself overcome; but they are not backward to notice the result of excess in the natives of the country. HENTZNER'S terse and simple observation, that beer 'is exceedingly well tasted, but strong, and what soon fuddles,' may, or may not, be founded upon his own personal experience. Dr. GEMELLI refers to 'Drink' in a similarly short and uncompromising vein: 'they fill themselves extravagantly with several sorts of liquors, as beer and ale, aqua vitæ, perry, mead, cider, mum, and usquebaugh, a violent burning drink.' This gentleman usually has the air of having found a new and hitherto undiscovered country. In

Foreign Visitors in England. 177

this remark he outdoes himself as a describer of savage life. As he proceeds, alluding to the custom of pledging the health, and its reputed origin, it is obvious that he regards the people as having not long since emerged from barbarism: 'In the time of the Danes, the English could not drink with safety, because while they were in that action the others basely murdered them; to prevent the which, every man desired his next neighbour, or the person he drank to, to defend and secure him during that time, against the malice of the others.'

The use of tobacco must have become very general in England after the Restoration. According to SORBIERE, 'scarce a day passes but a tradesman goes to the alehouse or tavern to smoke with some of his friends, and therefore public-houses are numerous here.'

After coffee-houses came into vogue, they increased in great numbers; they appeared to take the public taste, and most men had one or more to which they resorted. At the beginning of the eighteenth century, the coffee and chocolate houses were a constant *rendezvous* for men of business as well as idlers. Our visitors of that period are much taken with these fashionable places ; where besides coffee many other liquors were to be had ; where they smoked and gambled and read the *Gazette*, and discoursed freely about everything. Coffee-houses doubtless furnished the most agreeable opportunities for pastime of all sorts. MURALT notices that the national character could be well studied in such places, even by persons unacquainted with the language of the speakers. 'In my opinion' (he adds), ' they are very proper places to find people that a man has business with, or to pass away the time a little more agreeably, perhaps, than he can do at home. In other respects they are loathsome, full of smoke like a guard-room, and as much crowded. I believe 'tis these coffee-houses that furnish the inhabitants of this great city with slander, for there one hears exact accounts of everything done in town as if it were but a village.' He observes that it is common to see the clergy of London in coffee-houses, 'and even in taverns,' with pipes in their mouths.

CHAPTER XII.

Love of Sports. — Fighting and Wrestling. — Fox-hunting.

ANY of our friends deduce the national character from our national sports. The inherent fierceness of the English people is considered (and with some justice) to arise from the Danish element, with its hunting and predatory instincts, and from the Romans with their sanguinary displays in the arena. But, while thus reckoning us up, it does not appear difficult for some of them to take part as spectators in the more or less brutal exhibitions which London has always afforded. On the contrary, it is plain enough that they rather liked them than not. The average attendant on a bull-fight, or a cock-fight, may well be a Spaniard, or an Italian, or a

German. And it may be said to the credit of the French, that they, among all Europeans, have by far the least relish for barbarous diversions. There is a German Duke who comes to the bear-garden at Southwark; and 'in order to gratify his highness two bears and a bull were baited.' Then a Spanish grandee on another occasion is entertained with a pony-baiting, 'with an ape fastened on its back; and to see the animal kicking amongst the dogs, with the screams of the ape, beholding the curs hanging from the ears and neck of the pony, is *very laughable!*' When MISSON comes to notice the bear-garden sports, it is in a very matter-of-fact way; and if he has any lurking taste for the business, it is carefully disguised. He has personally no part in it; it is English, and that is enough. Anything that looks like fighting' (he says), 'is delicious to an Englishman. MISSON's item of *Sports and Diversions*, as a comment on this text, is a gem in its way. 'If two little boys quarrel in the street, the passengers stop, make a ring round them in a moment, and set them against one another, that they may come to fisticuffs. When 'tis come to a fight, each pulls off his neckcloth and his waistcoat, and gives them to hold to some of the bystanders; then they begin to brandish their fists in the air, the blows are aimed all at the face, they kick one another's shins, they tug one another by the hair. He that has got the other down may give him one blow or two before he rises, but no more; and let the boy get up ever so often, the other is obliged to box him again as often as he requires it. During the fight, the ring of bystanders encourages the combatants with great delight of heart, and never parts them while they fight according to the rules. And these bystanders are not only other boys, porters, and rabble, but all sorts of men of fashion, some thrusting by the mob that they may see plainly, others getting upon stalls, and all would hire places, if scaffolds could be built in a moment. The fathers and mothers of the boys let them fight on as well as the rest, and hearten him that gives the ground, or has the worst. These combats are less frequent among grown men than children, but they are not rare. If a coachman has a dispute about his fare with a gentleman that has hired him, and the gentleman offers to fight him to decide the quarrel, the coachman consents with all his heart. The gentleman pulls off his sword, lays it in some shop, with his cane, gloves, and cravat, and boxes in the same manner as I have described above. If the coachman gets soundly drubbed, which happens almost always, that goes for payment; but if he is the beator, the beatee must pay the money about which they quarrelled. I once saw the late Duke of Grafton at fisticuffs in the open street, with such a fellow, whom he lamb'd most horribly. In France we punish such rascals with our cane, and sometimes with the flat of the sword; but in England this is never practised. They use neither sword nor stick against a man that is unarmed, and if an unfortunate stranger (for an Englishman would never take it into his head) should draw his sword upon one that had none, he'd have a hundred people upon him in a moment, that would, perhaps, lay him so flat that he would hardly ever get up again until the Resurrection.

'Wrestling, too, is one of the diversions of the English, especially in the northern counties. Ringing of bells is one of their great delights, especially in the country. . . . In winter, football is a useful and charming exercise; it is a leather ball about as big as one's head, filled with wind; this is kicked about from one to another in the streets, by him that can get at it, and that is all the art of it.' There are numerous descriptions of prize-fighting and fencing-bouts, of a character which has long passed away. SORBIERE calls them fierce and brutish, and his account quite warrants his opinion. The Abbé LE BLANC observes that, in his time, these things were ceasing to be fashionable, and the only people who attend are but the lowest of the populace, or that class of men 'who are perhaps more despicable than the dregs of the people, because they imitate them as much in their manners, as they are exalted above them by their birth.' With regard to boxing, he presently adds, 'the nobility in

England do not excel in it less than the common people; one of the peers of the kingdom is at this day the terror of all the hackney coachmen in London.'

Fox-hunting and coursing come in for notice, even on the part of persons to whom the chase is an absolute novelty. The Abbé LE BLANC finds himself staying at a country-house near Stamford, in the midst of a people whose chief pleasure is hunting, in a nation where everybody loves it. For himself, the sound of the horn makes him willingly renounce the seclusion of his study. The violent passion of everybody for hunting infects his own spirit. He sees the clergyman and the lawyer, the justice of the peace and the farmer, leave everything for the chase. He finds expert horsewomen who are content to risk breaking their necks in order to serve a fresh opportunity for asserting their claims to be admired. He tells of a professor of mathematics who had the misfortune to lose his sight, and yet continued both his lessons on optics and his following of the hounds. Hunting the stag one day with fifty farmers in company, he notices an oddly-dressed man join in the chase, and finds that it was the post-boy, 'more intent upon his pleasure than concerned about the consequence of the letters he carried,' etc.

There is an anecdote related by one of the earlier travellers, by which he means to illustrate the extreme eagerness of the English for the chase, to the utter exclusion of any thought of danger. The armies of Henry VIII. and Francis being encamped near Terouanne, in Picardy, 'by some chance a fox sprang forth into the intermediate space. The English being, as was natural, emulous to take the fox, pursued it; the fox thereupon ran straight forward toward the army of the French; but the English, relaxing nothing, pursued it to the French encampment, and the latter, seeing the English coming impetuously toward them, issued forth and received them, and having put them to flight, as they were but few, they advanced still, pursuing them to their intrenchments.' In this scrimmage, the English are alleged to have lost more than two thousand men.

Monsieur GROSLEY regards it as a necessity that the English should foster the pursuits of hunting and racing. In common with most Frenchmen, he holds to the tradition of a settled melancholy in our natural disposition; and, assuming that this tradition is founded on fact, he is perhaps right in asserting that riding exercise is the best remedy, that it rouses the disposition with better effect than any other.

CHAPTER XIII.

The Drama and the Stage.

ROSLEY has much that is serious to say upon our melancholy. He puts it down to fogs, and to Protestantism; but he likewise considers all our amusements to be wanting in the elements of cheerfulness. The theatrical exhibitions in England he finds contributory to the national disorder. Our best comedies do not afford any relief against melancholy and dejection, with their useless complications and intrigues, which put the minds of those who endeavour to unravel them to the torture. As for the 'tragedies, which the people are most fond of, they consist of a number of bloody scenes, shocking to humanity; and these scenes are upon the stage as warm and affecting as the justest

action can render them : an action as lively, pathetic, and glowing, as that of their preachers is cold, languid, and uniform.' The most barbarous cruelty, and the most refined wickedness, are displayed in the representations of 'Macbeth, Richard the Third, King Lear, and other pieces of Shakespeare.' What those pieces want in point of regularity, is abundantly compensated by the choice of incidents of a nature most affecting, and most capable of harrowing up the soul. 'Most of their ancient kings act the part of fools, madmen, or idiots.' The last act of Richard the Third, with 'a crowd of princes and princesses poisoned, assassinated, stabbed,' rising from out of the earth to curse the sleeping tyrant, failed to interest him, and appeared to produce upon other spectators a quite different effect from what he had anticipated, in recollection of his perusal of a translation of the play. Neither is VOLTAIRE satisfied with the prospects of English tragedy as he saw it. Addison, he maintains, was the first English writer who composed a regular tragedy, and infused a spirit of elegance through every part. Shakespeare's great genius, natural and sublime, was such as, in time, to make his very faults venerable. Yet this writer's tragedies are but 'monstrous farces.' . . . 'Most of the whimsical, gigantic images of this poet have, through length of time, acquired a right of passing for sublime. Most of the modern dramatic writers have copied him; but the touches and descriptions which are applauded in Shakespeare, are hissed at in these writers. . . . Dramatic writers don't consider that they should not imitate him; and the ill-success of Shakespeare's imitators produces no other effect than to make him be considered as inimitable.' VOLTAIRE'S point of view appears to be the gross want of taste implied in mixing up humour with tragic scenes, as in 'Hamlet,' where 'two gravediggers make a grave, and are all the time drinking, singing ballads, and making humorous reflections on the several skulls they throw up with their spades,' and in 'Julius Cæsar,' with the 'jokes of the Roman shoemakers and cobblers introduced in the same scene with Brutus and Cassius.' He gives Otway's 'Venice Preserved' as an example of a good tragedy utterly spoiled by the introduction of some buffoonery, 'calculated merely for the dregs of the people,' which the actors speedily struck out from the play.

Other of our intelligent visitors notice this frequent defect. It appears to them so necessary for the English to be sad and gay in quick return. Both plays and actors are 'a mixture of the comic and the serious'; melancholy and merriment follow one another. 'Oroonoko' is mentioned as a play remarkable for true and pathetic pictures, yet it could never be endured in France, because of the low comedy intermixed. In fine, English tragedies were held to be true to nature, but wanting in dignity; ruined by ill-timed horse-play and buffoonery.

The comedies of the seventeenth and eighteenth centuries would have been more highly appreciated had they been less often 'stuffed with rant and obscenity.' MURALT considers that the comedies which he read, or saw acted, were a source of corruption to society; that young people were familiarized with vice as an indifferent affair, and not as Vice. Idle stories, he says, and swearing scenes, go down better than anything else. Another visitor notices that the English stage is disgraced by the representation of thieves; and remarks that it is shameful that the 'Beggar's Opera' should so long entertain the Londoners. There is much complaint that Molière is so constantly plagiarized by English playwrights. But VOLTAIRE holds that Wycherley's 'Misanthrope' will bear comparison with its prototype for strength and boldness; 'although they are less delicate, and the rules of decorum are not so well observed.' His opinion of Congreve is very high, as one who raised the glory of comedy beyond any English writer before or since his time.

The performance of low comedy was considered to be in a much more natural manner than in France; otherwise, English players came 'very short of the French.' There were some comedians who were excellent, but any below the first rank were miserably bad. Buffoons were more frequently to be seen than tolerable actors. 'The English love caricatures; they are more struck with a large face and a great nose, than with a noble and graceful countenance.' The comic characters were always overstrained. The more the comedian found of caricature in his part, the more he seemed to think there should be in his action—grimaces served him better than vocal modulation.

There are many curious experiences of the London stage scattered up and down our visitors' stories of the first half of the eighteenth century. Here is one, by the Abbé LE BLANC, which forcibly accounts for the views above recited. A play is produced, which it was known beforehand was to be damned by the 'first-nighters' of the period: 'Half an hour before the play was to begin, the spectators gave notice of their dispositions by frightful hisses and outcries, equal, perhaps, to what were ever heard in a Roman amphitheatre. I could not have known, but by my eyes only, that I was among an

Foreign Visitors in England.

assembly of beings who thought themselves to be reasonable. The author, who had foreseen the fury of the pit, took care to be armed against it. He knew what people he had to deal with; and, to make them easy, put in his prologue double the usual dose of incense that is offered to their vanity. . . . This precaution succeeded; the charms of flattery, more strong than those of music, deprived them of all their fierceness.

'The author, having by flattery begun to tame this wild audience, proceeded entirely to reconcile it by the first scene of his performance. Two actors came in, one dressed in the English manner very decently, and the other with black eyebrows, a riband an ell long under his chin, a big peruke immoderately powdered, and his nose all bedaubed with snuff. What Englishman could not know a Frenchman by this ridiculous picture? The common people of London think we are indeed such sort of folks, and of their own accord add to our real follies all that their authors are pleased to give us. But when it was found that the man thus equipped, being also laced down every seam of his coat, was nothing but a cook, the spectators were equally charmed and surprised. The author had taken care to make him speak all the impertinences he could devise: and, for that reason, all the impertinences of his farce were excused, and the merit of it immediately decided. There was a long criticism upon our manners, our customs, and, above all, our cookery. The excellence and virtues of English beef were cried up; and the author maintained that it was owing to the qualities of its juice that the English were so courageous, and had such a solidity of understanding, which raised them above all the nations in Europe. He preferred the noble old English pudding beyond all the finest ragouts that were ever invented by the greatest geniuses that France has produced; and all these ingenious strokes were loudly clapped by the audience. The pit forgot that they came to damn the play. . . . Intractable as the populace appear in this country, those who know how to take hold of their foibles may easily carry their point.'

CHAPTER XIV.

Literature.—The Fine Arts.—The Royal Society.

T will readily be supposed that some of these writers were as deeply interested in the existing state and prospects of English literature.

VOLTAIRE, who made himself as much of an Englishman as was possible during the time he was here, proclaims that learning was held in greater honour in England than in his own country. He ascribes much of the English desire for the cultivation of the mind to the freedom of our institutions. In England (he says), the governments of Greece and Rome are the subject of every conversation, so that every man is under the necessity of perusing such authors as treat of them . . . and this study leads naturally to that of polite literature. The people in general are indispensably obliged to cultivate their understandings, seeing that everyone enjoys the liberty of publishing his thoughts with regard to public affairs. In common with other visitors of the period, VOLTAIRE rejoices to note the great honour given in England to persons of distinguished mental gifts, and how literary merit is often the stepping-stone to public employment. The instances of Addison, Swift, Prior, Newton, are put forward as triumphant comparison with the state of things in France. LE BLANC adduces an ingenious reason—which may, perhaps, have considerable truth in it—for the spread of literary taste in this country. He says that we are a people whose leisure is more burthensome to us than is commonly seen with our neighbours : 'For the English do not live and converse so much with one another as the French; wherefore, to fill up the vacuity of their lives, they are obliged to read or do nothing. . . . They are naturally inclined to silence, as we are to exhaust ourselves in discourse; and silence inspires a taste for reading, as much as talkativeness is averse to it. Perhaps even a great many persons, who in this country write books, would never have attempted any such employment if they had had spirits enough to do anything else.'

It is considered a grave disadvantage that the 'suggestions of Dryden, Locke, and Swift to found an English Academy did not bear fruit.' VOLTAIRE considers that it would have been of more benefit to literature than the French Academy, which immensely improved its language, and fostered the *belles lettres*. As the establishment of the Royal Society gave a great impulse to scientific inquiry, an Academy of English would have introduced methods into the pursuits of literature which would have been of incalculable benefit. It is suggested by LE BLANC, indeed, that the English do not know how to make a book. While a Frenchman devotes all his arts to good methods, and can 'range a number of nothings' into the most delightful and perfect order, it is rare to find English treatises that are not almost destitute of method; books full of most excellent matter, but clumsily put together. 'The English, who treat of the abstract sciences, are not solicitous enough to express themselves clearly; they seem always afraid of saying too much, and are as sparing of words as they are prodigal of ideas. Such is the character of the immortal Bacon. . . . Locke is, perhaps, the only English author who knew how to avoid this fault. Those, on the contrary, who write upon subjects of taste and entertainment, run too much into diffuseness and redundance; they are always afraid they do not show wit enough, and continue to crowd figures upon figures. Every moment they fly from their subject, that they may not omit the least trifles which have any relation to it; so that the principal idea is often clouded by the multitude of ideas that are accessory.' This writer alleges that there was no good dictionary of English in his time, 'and hardly a tolerable grammar.'

It is remarked by these writers, as a matter to provoke surprise, that eloquence in declamation was at a very low standard, seeing the opportunities that the institutions of the country afford for its cultivation and exercise. With some parliamentary exceptions, our ancestors of two hundred years past would seem to have been lamentably deficient in the art of public speaking. The pulpit oratory is represented as a most tedious monotony; its substance tinged with 'mere pedantry.' The art of reading aloud was marked with affectation and personal peculiarities. And when they happen, in reading, to go out of prose into verse, 'you would swear you no longer heard the same person.'

The condition and prospects of the fine arts, at this period, must have been very degraded, to judge from the criticisms passed by Frenchmen reporting on them to their countrymen. The English are held, in point of fact, to have literally no taste at all. They had no painter before Hogarth, and his truth to nature was 'too true.' Painting and sculpture appeared to be either unknown, or but in their infancy. The statues erected in public places in London are dismal; that of Queen Anne in St. Paul's Churchyard looks 'as if she were holding a wax taper, and doing public penance.' The equestrian statue of Charles I., at Charing Cross, is the least deserving of reprobation. Madame BOCAGE is very short and incisive on the point: The heroes, to whose honour the City of London erects statues, shine only by their reputation, and not by the ability of the sculptors.' LE BLANC is as sarcastic over the painters: Sir James Thornhill he regards as the only English painter who could dare to aspire to the kind of decoration attempted in the dome of St. Paul's Cathedral; and even here you 'would be puzzled to decide not in what part he has excelled, but that in which he has been less faulty.' This is a kind of painting (he proceeds) which requires 'a genius that Nature has refused him.' Even the portrait-painters do not deserve to be named: they 'have practised this noble profession as the meanest trade, for money alone, without the least ambition of fame.'

There is a general agreement of opinion as to the excellence of artisanship in England. Its reputation appears to have already extended over all parts of Europe. It is remarked by one of our friends that the English artisan has 'the quality, peculiar to him, never to swerve from the degree of perfection in his trade which he is master of; whatever he undertakes he does as well as he can.' On the same grounds it is acknowledged, on all hands, that the progress of the English in the exact sciences—'in the sciences grounded on calculations, and the arts that depend on the rule and compass'—surpassed that of other countries. GROSLEY brings up his favourite topic of melancholy as the motive power; and considers that the abstruseness of these pursuits requires that the whole soul should bury itself in its subject—hence the aptitude of the English. The labours which lead to great discoveries, he says, were in all ages the lot of melancholy tempers. However that may be, it was universally admitted that England had long led the way in experimental philosophy. Bacon and Newton are deeply reverenced by our intelligent friends. VOLTAIRE passes a high eulogium on these great men: 'the equal of Sir Isaac Newton is hardly found in a thousand years;' and does not fail to seize the opportunity of propounding his favourite text: 'The smallness of these illustrious persons who enslave their fellow-creatures, as compared with those who enable us to read the secrets of the universe.'

The leading cause of the impulse given to scientific inquiry in the middle of the seventeenth century is put down to 'the long eclipse of the monarchy.' SORBIERE'S special acquaintances in England were scientific men, many of them 'persons of quality,' as he calls them, who, having no court to make, applied themselves instead to study; 'some turning their heads to chymistry, others to mathematics, or natural philosophy —the King himself having been so far from being neglectful of these things that he has attained to so much knowledge as made me astonished, when I had audience of his Majesty.' We owe to SORBIERE, and to the writer of COSMO's journal, some interesting references to the early days of the Royal Society. Charles II. made it a special object of his care, and became its patron; not so much to give dignity and encouragement to the society, as because of his taste for scientific pursuits, and his extensive knowledge of some branches. The founders of the society did 'all for honour, and nothing to advance the fortunes of its members.' The subscription was heavy, for the society spared no expense in the collection of rarities, and in the making of experiments. Although of thoroughly aristocratic origin, there was a studious effort always made to ensure equality, and give precedence to no one. Respect was offered to every man, whatever his station in life, English or foreigner, if he made any observation which he thought worthy the attention of the society. GROSLEY (who was himself elected a member) was once present when a joiner, in his workman's dress, laid before the society a method which he had invented to explain the causes of the ebbing and flowing of the tides. He spoke a long time, without knowing much of the subject; yet he was listened to with the utmost attention, 'thanked for his confidence in the knowledge of the society, requested to digest his ideas to writing, or cause them to be digested for him, and was accompanied to the door by one of the members.' SORBIERE was one of the earliest foreigners elected into the Royal Society. He thought it doing him great honour. He had been secretary to a similar academy in Paris, and had some pretensions to be considered a modern philosopher. SORBIERE'S references to the etiquette observed at the meetings of the society arouse interesting reflections when one recollects that the age of unlimited deference to rank and wealth was passing away: 'The president sits at the middle of the table in an easy-chair. . . . All the other members take their places as they think fit, and without any ceremony; and if anyone comes in after the society is fixed, nobody stirs, but he takes a place presently where he can find it, that so no interruption may be given to him that speaks. . . . There is nobody here eager to speak, that makes a long harangue, or intent upon saying all he knows. A speaker is never interrupted; and differences of opinion cause no manner of resentment. Nothing seemed to me more civil, respectful, and better managed than this meeting; and if there are any private discourses held between any while a member is speaking, they only whisper, and the least sign from the president causes a sudden stop, though they have not told their mind out.'

CHAPTER XV.

'The greatest beauties in the world.'

OUR travellers are universally gallant. They are mostly surprised to see so much liberty allowed to womenkind. The saying is often repeated that England is 'the paradise of women, and the purgatory of horses,' because the females are almost like masters, and the horses are worked harder than in any other country. Even the captious PERLIN relents over the ladies, and declares that Englishwomen are 'the greatest beauties in the world, and as fair as alabaster . . . they are also cheerful and courteous, and of a good address.' RATHGEB, diarist of the Duke Frederick of Wirtemberg, is less carried away by their dazzling qualities of mind and person, than concerned with the extreme amount of liberty they enjoy, 'which they know well how to make use of, for they go dressed out in exceedingly fine clothes, and give all their attention to their cuffs and stuffs, to such a degree indeed that many a one does not hesitate to wear velvet in the streets, which is common with them, whilst at home they have not a piece of dry bread.'

The Dutch historian, VAN METEREN, who lived here many years during the sixteenth century, thus discourses in much the same vein : 'Wives in England are entirely in the power of their husbands, their lives only excepted. But although the women there are entirely in the power of their husbands except for their lives, yet they are not kept so strictly as they are in Paris and elsewhere. Nor are they shut up, but they have the free management of the housekeeping after the fashion of those of the Netherlands. . . . They go to market to buy what they like best to eat. They are well-dressed, fond of taking it easy, and commonly leave the care of household matters and drudgery to their servants. They sit before their doors, decked out in fine clothes, in order to see and be seen by the passers-by. In all banquets and feasts they are shown the greatest honour; they are placed at the upper end of the table, where they are the first served. . . . All the rest of the time they employ in walking or riding, in playing at cards or otherwise, in visiting their friends and keeping company, conversing with their equals and their neighbours, and making merry with them at childbirths, christenings, churchings, and funerals; and all this with the permission and knowledge of their husbands, as such is the custom. England is called the paradise of married women. The girls who are not yet married are kept much more rigorously and strictly than in the Low Countries.' Baron VON POLLNITZ also alludes to the disposition to gad about on the part of women who are not obliged, or have not the disposition, to be more usefully employed. 'The ladies here,' he says, 'have little to employ them, their amusement being to give and receive visits, to go often to court, to have the pleasure of being seen, which really is of all pleasures that which they seem to take mos delight in. . . . They turn out of a morning with a black velvet mask on their faces, a coif on in form of a hat, with the brims down, a round gown, and a white apron, and in this trim they go to the park or where else they please.' Yet the Baron, one of the gayest of the gay, and hero of a hundred amours, is deeply smitten, be their weaknesses what they may: 'They have in my opinion such an air of modesty and good-nature, and withal such a bashful simplicity, as charm me; and such tender languishing eyes, too, as, though not universally pleasing, yet captivate me to such a degree that if I was but twenty years of age, I should have gone very much astray. Most of the English-women are handsome, they have the finest hair in the world, and are only obliged to pure nature for their complexions. It is a pleasure to see them blush,' etc. Epithets are profuse, indeed, on female charms in England: 'Of marvellous beauty and wonderfully clever.' . . . 'Charming, modest, handsome, and unaffected.' . . . 'By nature so mighty pretty, as I have scarce ever beheld, for they do not falsify, paint or bedaub themselves as in Italy or in other places; but they are somewhat awkward in their style of dress, for they dress in splendid stuffs, and many a one wears three cloth gowns or petticoats, one over the other.' . . . Dr. GEMELLI says: 'The women are very beautiful and genteel, and courteous of behaviour, being in short looked upon as one of the valuable things which England affords, which are:

'*Anglia mons, pons, fons, ecclesia, fœmina, lana.* . . .

Add to this commendation that they do whatsoever they please, and do so generally wear the breeches (as we use to say), that it is now become a proverb that England is the hell of horses and the paradise of women; and if there were a bridge from the island to the continent, all the women in Europe would run thither.'

The Prince of Tuscany made himself very agreeable to the fair sex. He would readily escape into their society, and loved to see them on parade in the parks. He had himself suffered matrimonial shipwreck; but that misfortune had by no means made him a woman-hater. Count MAGALOTTI, his secretary and chronicler, was not less impressionable. This writer's account of Englishwomen is excellently given. 'The women of London,' he says, 'are not inferior to the men either in stature or in beauty, for they are all of them handsome, and for the most part tall, with black eyes, abundance of light-coloured hair, and a neatness which is extreme, their only personal defect being their teeth, which are not, generally speaking, very white. They live with all the liberty that the custom of the country authorizes. This custom dispenses with that rigorous constraint and reservedness which are practised by the women of other countries, and they go whithersoever they please, either alone, or in company; and those of the lower order frequently go so far as to play at ball publicly in the streets. They are very fond of paying respect to foreigners, and in society show them a vast deal of courtesy and attention. The slightest possible introduction is sufficient to be admitted to their conversation, on the same terms as their countrymen and relations, who, on their part, behave to them with the greatest modesty, holding female honour in the highest respect and veneration. So great is the respect which the English entertain for their women, that in their houses the latter govern everything despotically, making themselves feared by the men, courageous as they are on other occasions.' MISSON is almost always certain to say something surprisingly different from what other people do. The present case is not an exception, for he maintains that women in England have 'neither so much favour nor so much honour, as their beauty, their graceful mien, their genteelness, and so many charms as they are possessed of, might justly challenge.'

Monsieur GROSLEY is philosophically verbose over the English ladies. He finds them so sensible of their beauty, that they are little solicitous about artificial adornments, excepting at public assemblies. Then,

Foreign Visitors in England. 213

with their diamonds and lace they indeed make a distinguished figure. He attributes much of their beauty, and with unquestionable truth, to the frequency of outdoor exercise. GROSLEY has heard of the despotic power alleged to be held by Englishwomen, and in the course of his inquiries an incident occurs which appears to throw some light on the matter. At a certain evening assembly, he was asked by a lady whether he had exhausted the curiosities and objects of observation furnished by the metropolis. 'I made answer that there was still one of great importance for me to know, and that she and her company could give me all the information I desired: this was, whether in England the husband or the wife governed the house? My question being explained to all the ladies present, they discussed it, and amused themselves with it, and the answer which they agreed should be returned to me was, that husbands alone could resolve me. I then proposed it to the husbands, who with one voice declared that they durst not decide. The perplexity discovered by those gentlemen gave me the solution I desired.' We have a signal exception to this generally flattering tone, in the report of the Swiss MURALT. He is not so deeply impressed with the beauty of Englishwomen. 'They have all fair hair and beautiful fair faces, but without any sprightliness.' Out of a hundred handsome women, he finds scarce ten that are agreeable-looking. What pleases him most is 'their modesty, and a gentle bashfulness that makes them easily blush, and cast down their eyes every minute.' . . . 'As for their humour, they are taken to be gentle, frank, and easy, at first reserved, but soon growing familiar, even to a degree of playing the fool; hasty in anger; lazy, and accustomed to idleness. . . . From their idleness proceeds their uneasiness, their curiosity to know things to come, their fondness of fortune-telling, and their credulity.'

One of the short essays comprised in LE BLANC'S account of England is principally devoted to *conversation with the fair sex.* The subject is treated in a particularly judicious tone. In his time, it was doubtless true that female society was comparatively neglected, except in frivolous pastime. 'The English lose a great deal,' he points out, 'in conversing so little with the sex whom nature has endowed with the graces; and whose company has constant charms, and a certain sweetness not to be found in men. . . . Their presence and conversation polishes and softens men, and by the habit acquired of endeavouring to please them, a more agreeable tone of voice is contracted. . . . But the English seem to fear the company of women, as much as the French delight in it —they think the fair sex are made only to take possession of their hearts, and seldom or never to afford any amusement to their minds. They prefer the pleasure of toasting their healths in a tavern, to that of chatting with them in a circle.' Alluding to the excuse made that the women in England are not so amusing as in France, he does not hesitate to lay the blame upon the men, whose 'dangerous habit of drinking destroys the delicacy of sentiments, and perhaps even the desire of pleasing.' However, thanks to a later generation, boasting of its Barbauld, its Wollstonecraft, its Edgeworth, these things now belong to antiquity.

INDEX.

ADDISON, Joseph, as a dramatist, 188
Ale and beer extolled, 29, 175
American visitors, 107, 111, 131 *et seq.*
Artisans, foreign, in England, 41
Artisanship of the English, 201

Bassompierre, Marshal de, his embassy to England, x., 9
Bear-garden sports, 180
Beaumont, ambassador in England, 33, 34
Beckett's shrine at Canterbury, 60
Beer, 29, 46, 175
Boxing, 183
Boyle, Robert, visited by Cosmo III., 13-15
Bread, good quality of English, 166
Brougham, Lord, notice of, 108
Brown, Rawdon, his labours in the Venetian archives, 7
Buffoonery on the English stage, 190 *et seq.*
Burke, Edmund, notice of, 113

Canning, George, notice of, 108
Canterbury, co. Kent, 49, 60-62
Carus, C. G., xv.
Character of the English people, 122 *et seq.*
Charles I., 5, 101
Charles II. entertains Cosmo III., 9 *et seq.*
   ,,   his scientific turn, 17, 203
   ,,   his courtesy, 22, 24
   ,,   his recreations, 84
   ,,   his character, 101
Charles V., Emperor, his reception in England, 4
Cheapside, 71
Chelmsford, co. Essex, reception of Marie de Medicis, 5
Christmas pudding, 163
Civility of the English, 135
Coffee and chocolate houses, 178
Comedies of Congreve and others, 191
Cookery in England, 24, 161 *et seq.*

Coronation Stone, 80
Cosmo III., Prince of Tuscany, xi., 9 *et seq.*
Cyder, 175

Daryl, Philippe, his 'Public Life in England,' xvi., 118, 119
Dinners of the English, 161, 163
Dover, co. Kent, 28, 31
Drake, Sir Francis, his ship *Golden Hind*, 67
Drama in England, 187 *et seq.*
Drinking customs, 46, 53, 167 *et seq.*
Du Bocage, Mme., xiii.

Edward IV., his court at Windsor, 91
Eldon, Lord, notice of, 110
Elizabeth, Queen, her court at Greenwich, 94
English character, 122 *et seq.*
Englishwomen, 206, 216
Esquiros, Alphonse, xvi.
Exeter, co. Devon, 10, 11

Fashions brought from France, 37
Fighting, 'delicious to an Englishman,' 180 *et seq.*
Fine Arts in England, 199
Fogs of London, 75
Food and feeding, 160 *et seq.*
Football described, 183
Foreign visitors, their various characteristics, 3, 123
    ,,   ,,   their treatment in England, 29 *et seq.*
Fox, Charles James, notice of, 112
Fox-hunting, 184
Freedom of manners, 103
Frenchmen in London, 29, 30, 35

Gardens, celebrated, 83, 86
Garter, Order of the, 18
Gemelli-Careri, Dr. J., xii.
Giovius, Paulus, his estimate of the English people, 40
Giustinian, Venetian ambassador, viii., 6, 61
Goldsmiths' shops in London, 73
Gravesend, co. Kent, 47, 64
Greenwich, co. Kent, 67, 94
Grey, Earl, notice of, 110
Grosley, Pierre Jean, visitor from Troyes, xiv., *passim*

Hampton Court, 20, 90
Hawthorne, Nathaniel, in England, xv., 132
Henry VIII., his magnificent receptions, 4, 6

Index.

Hentzner, Paul, visitor at the court of Elizabeth, ix., 47, 62 *et seq.*, 94
Hoppin, James M., xvi.

Innkeeper 'boycotted' for extortion, 49
Inns and innkeepers, 47 *et seq.*
'Jacob's pillow' at Westminster Abbey, 80
James I., his hospitality, 8
James II., 19, 21, 101, 102
Jorevin, his adventures in England, xi., 43, 44 *et seq.*, 53

Kent, the county extolled, 59, 64
King, Lord, notice of, 110
King's evil, Charles II. touching for, 17

La Gruthuyse, Louis de Bruges Seigneur de, viii.
La Motraye, xiii., his praise of Kent, 60
La Serre, Sieur de, x.
Le Blanc, Abbé, xiii., notices of England, *passim*
Lemnius, ix., his friendly experiences, 40, 137
Liberty idolized in England, 104, 105
Literature and learning, 195
London, Corporation of, 6, 21, 34
  ,,   notes on, 69, *et seq.*
London Bridge, 64

Magalotti, Count, secretary to Cosmo III., notices by, 14, 18, 24
  ,,   ,, his summary of the English character, 138
Marie de Medicis, Queen, 5, 26
Meteren, Van, Dutch historian, ix., on the English people, 137
Misson, xii., notices of England, *passim*
Monk, General, 25
Moritz, C. F., his walking-tour in England, xiv., 54 *et seq.*
  ,,   his notes on the House of Commons, 112
Muralt, xii., 214

New Exchange, in the Strand, 71
Nicander Nucius, ix., at the Tower, 70
Northampton, 50, 51
Norwich, foreign settlers in, 42

Otway, Thomas, dramatist, 190

Palaces, Royal, 83 *et seq.*
Parliament, Houses of, 107-15
Pastry, English, 162
Patriotism an important attribute of the English, 126
Pedestrian travellers, 54, 55
Perlin, Etienne, ix., his estimate of the English people, 40

Perlin, Etienne, notes on drinking, 171
Philip II., his complaints of the populace, 38
Pitt, William, notice of, 111
Politics, 104 *et seq.*
Pollnitz, notes of England, xiii., *passim*
Pückler-Muskan, Prince von, xv.
Puddings, 165

Raumer, Von, xv., on English politics, 119
    ,,   ,,   on Sabbatarianism, 153
Refugees settled in England, 35, 41, 42
Religion in England, 142, 154 *et seq.*
Richmond Palace, 88

Royal Exchange, 71
Royal Society, 197, 202, *et seq.*
Rozmital, Von, viii., his summary of the English character, 137

St. James's Park, 83-85
St. Paul's Cathedral, 75-77
Sculpture in London, 200
Sea-sickness, 26-28
Sectarianism, 142 *et seq.*
Shakespeare, William, criticisms on, 188, 189
Shops in London, 72, 73
Silliman, Benjamin, xiv.
Simond, Louis, xv., on English notions of freedom, 105
Sittingbourne, co. Kent, 47
Social intercourse deficient in England, 147, 148
Somerset House (old), 66
Sorbière, Samuel, x., notices of England, *passim*
Sovereigns of England, 100
Sports, national, 179
Stowmarket, co. Suffolk, adventure there, 45
Street-brawls, 32, 43, 181, 182
Suicide, our alleged tendency to, 146
Sully, Duke of, ix., his first day in London, 32
Sunday, its absurdly strict observance, 151 *et seq.*
Swans on the Thames, 65

Taine, H., xvi., his arrival in London, 158
Thames River, 63 *et seq.*
Theatrical performances, 188
Theobalds Palace, 86
Thorndon Hall, co. Essex, 24
Toast-drinking, 168 *et seq.*
Tobacco-smoking, 53, 156, 177
Tower of London, 69

Index. 221

Tragedies of Shakespeare and others, 188
Trevisano, Andrea, viii.

Voltaire, xiii.

Walloon refugees, 42
Wellington, Duke of, notice, 109
Westminster Abbey, 77-79
Westminster Election (1782), notice of, 116
Whitehall Palace, 83, 89
Windsor Castle, 18, 56, 87, 90, 91
Women, their favoured condition in England, 207 *et seq.*
Wrestling, 183